Contents

Contributors

Susan Brown – Head of the Political Analysis Programme, Institute for Justice and Reconciliation.

Alex Boraine – Chairperson of the Board of Directors, International Center for Transitional Justice, New York.

Sue de Villiers – Independent Researcher and Editor in the area of Human Rights.

John Darby – Professor of Comparative Ethnic Studies at the Kroc Institute, University of Notre Dame.

Erik Doxtader – Assistant Professor of Rhetoric, University of Wisconsin (Madison), USA and Senior Research Fellow, Institute for Justice and Reconciliation.

Mieke Holkeboer – Former Research Fellow, Institute for Justice and Reconciliation.

Antjie Krog – Extraordinary Professor, University of the Western Cape, Poet and Journalist.

Funekile Magilindane – Intern in the Politcical Analysis Programme, Institute for Justice and Reconciliation.

Dani W Nabudere – Executive Director, Afrika Study Center Mbale, Uganda, and Senior Research Fellow, Institute for Justice and Reconciliation.

Fiona Ross – Lecturer, Department of Social Anthropology, University of Cape Town.

Jeremy Sarkin – Senior Professor of Law, University of the Western Cape.

Ronald Slye – Associate Professor, Seattle University School of Law.

Zola Sonkosi – Executive Consultant, Institute for Justice and Reconciliation.

Charles Villa-Vicencio – Executive Director, Institute for Justice and Reconciliation.

PIECES OF THE PUZZLE

Keywords on
Reconciliation
and Transitional
Justice

Edited by Charles Villa-Vicencio and Erik Doxtader
Preface by Richard Goldstone

Published by the Institute for Justice and Reconciliation
46 Rouwkoop Road, Rondebosch 7700, Cape Town, South Africa
www.ijr.org.za

ISBN: 0-9584794-5-3

Produced by Compress   www.compress.co.za

Marketing and sales agent: Oneworldbooks
www.oneworldbooks.com
Distributed by BlueWeaver
Orders to be placed with Blue Weaver
PO Box 30370, Tokai 7966, Cape Town, South Africa
Fax: +27 21 701 7302
E-mail: orders@blueweaver.co.za

This publication was generously
supported by the W K Kellogg Foundation

Preface

The essays contained in this collection cover a wide field. They demonstrate the growth industry that transitional justice has become during the past three decades. This is, of course, a reason for rejoicing. It reflects the significant number of nations that have moved from dictatorship and oppression to freedom and democracy. It is only in that context that transitional justice becomes relevant.

Rather than repeat the substance of these essays, I propose in this preface to place my own gloss on some of the issues they raise. The first is the relationship between peace and justice. It is not sufficiently appreciated that the jurisdiction of the United Nations Security Council to establish the two ad hoc international criminal tribunals for the former Yugoslavia and Rwanda depended on this linkage. The Security Council is only able to issue peremptory and binding resolutions under Chapter VII of the United Nations Charter. Those provisions are only triggered by the Council's determination that a particular situation constitutes a threat to international peace and security. Having done so, it can impose its will upon all member states in resolutions designed to remove such a threat. It can adopt measures short of military force such as blockades, embargos and sanctions. Or it can resort to military action.

In the case of both the former Yugoslavia and Rwanda, the Security Council established criminal tribunals as a form of peace-making. In doing so it was compelled to recognise, correctly I would suggest, that there is a direct link between justice and peace. And, by peace, I have in mind not some short-term ceasefire or armistice, but an enduring peace. And, by justice, I have in mind not only criminal prosecutions, but also mechanisms such as truth and reconciliation commissions (TRCs).

I would suggest, further, that much of the violence that has caused such misery and chaos in so many regions of the globe could be ascribed to the absence of forms of justice and the presence of national amnesia with regard to egregious human rights violations.

Ignoring the victims of such abuses too frequently results in bitterness, hatred and calls for revenge. When those calls are unrequited, they provide the toxic fuel available to evil leaders. That was certainly the experience in the Balkans and Rwanda.

The second aspect I would emphasise is the crucial importance of restoring the human dignity that oppression and (especially) racism robs from its victims. Serious human rights violations are not perpetrated against people who are regarded as being on the same level as the perpetrators. They are thus associated with dehumanising the victims in order to justify the cruelty imposed upon them. As is pointed out by some of the contributors, transitional justice must be associated with the restoration of the dignity of the victims. And that should by no means be confused with patronising them. Their equality and intrinsic worth as human beings has to be both recognised and demonstrated. They must be assisted in regaining their own pride and feelings of self-worth.

With regard to the South African TRC, I would suggest that perhaps its greatest gift to our people is the common history of the apartheid-era that it has produced. Without the TRC, there would have been at least two 'histories' of our dark past. There would have been a black history, the history of the victims. That would have approximated the truth, for victims know first hand what befell them. Black South Africans experienced daily the indignity and cruelty of racial oppression. The white history would have been one of denial. Perpetrators always put out denials and the beneficiaries of their evil policies feel more comfortable with those denials even when they lack credibility. The outpouring of evidence from both victims and perpetrators who appeared before the TRC effectively put an end to these fabrications. Future generations of South African children will learn the same history in our schools, and this provides a solid foundation for breaking down the inequality and inequity that still endures in our nation.

Associated with this enormous benefit of the TRC is the need to roll out human rights education. Human rights can only be realised and enjoyed by people who understand and appreciate them. Bills of Rights and egalitarian democratic constitutions are worth little if the people who are their intended beneficiaries are not taught to appreciate the essence of those rights. I would suggest that too little attention is given to this essential role of teachers in emerging democracies.

In South Africa, we are fortunate that the institutions of democracy were established by the minority white rulers of our land. They had regular elections, a legislature and an independent judiciary. Those institutions have been taken over by the duly elected representatives of all South Africans and they are operating with a vigour previously unknown. I need refer in this regard only to the rapidly transforming judiciary and to the independence of the committees of Parliament. The survivors of oppression in the states of the former Soviet Union did not have the benefit of those institutions and had to invent them – a far more daunting prospect.

For societies in transition, time is usually more an enemy than a friend. The ceasefire in Sri Lanka is imperilled by the unconscionably long time the leaders of that beautiful island are taking to make real and meaningful progress in their peace negotiations. The same holds true of Bosnia, Herzegovina and Kosovo. If there is no sense of urgency, the opportunities for peace will be squandered. This is also an area of transition that deserves more empirical research.

In conclusion, I would suggest that all South Africans rejoice in their remarkable achievements. My hope is that other societies looking to our successes will capture the essence of our transition – the many aspects that are described in this collection of essays. I would like to conclude this preface with the words of Dani Nabudere in his essay on *ubuntu*:

> The global community of the 21st century can draw inspiration from excavating the depths of African philosophy for the benefit of all humanity. In this way, it may be possible for Africa to claim the 21st century to be an African century and the African Renaissance to be a humanising experience for humanity.

That is wonderful challenge and aspiration. Transitional justice is ultimately about nations torn apart by gross violations of human rights learning to live together within a context of dignity, human rights and social justice.

Richard Goldstone
Fordham University
New York

Introduction

Reconciliation is not intuitive and it is not easy. As both a process and goal, its power must be cultivated and nurtured. In the most fragile of circumstances, reconciliation calls adversaries to create common ground in the midst of bitter memory and ongoing conflict. Such efforts take time, and they are frequently painful. It is a task that can be guided but not directed. Addressed to bridging deep division, reconciliation seeks to deliver an inclusive or holistic notion of justice that stresses both accountability for past wrongs and the need for future, peaceful co-existence. Reconciliation and justice thus struggle to chart the course forward, turning the wounds of the past into the basis for learning to live together within the rule of law and in pursuit of a culture of human rights.

There is now substantial debate over the nature of reconciliation and transitional justice. In international and local arenas, this debate frequently addresses the question of what can and needs to happen in that period of time that sits between the often catastrophic conflict marred by atrocity and war, and the beginning of a democratic process of peace-making and socio-economic reconstruction.

The problem of how to best move from past to future does not have an easy answer. At a basic level, the pursuit of reconciliation and retributive justice is about creating and maintaining a balance between preventing the re-ignition of violence and socio-political change that is supported by the rule of law, the affirmation of human rights and democratic governance. The line is a fine one. On the one hand, retributive justice initiatives succeed only insofar as they are contextually sensitive and politically realistic. On the other, such programmes cannot forgo or forget legal and moral ideals, goods that may seem distant in the crucible of radical political change.

In transitional situations, the immediate submission to certain demands, whether these be the right of victims of gross human rights violations to see the prosecution of those responsible for their suffering, the provision of comprehensive reparations, the redress of socio-economic inequality, or the granting of amnesty to political and military leaders, may risk undermining fragile peace accords and thwarting efforts to stabilise new democratic institutions and promote human rights. Not all of these needs can be met while some cannot be met at all. These limitations, however, cannot excuse inaction, naïve idealism or undue delay in righting the wrongs that divide transitional societies. Reconciliation and transitional justice initiatives have to make a difference and they need to do so in a principled manner.

In attempting to move beyond autocratic rule and violence and toward a sustainable peace, transitional justice initiatives must balance a number of specific needs. These include:

- The affirmation of human rights ideals *and* a concern to ensure that a society in transition does not relapse into civil war.
- The need to hold human rights offenders legally accountable for their actions *and* to open the possibility for them to participate in the creation of a new society.
- The need to address the requirements of individual victims *and* the need to take account of communal needs, social services and collective development.
- The need for reparations *and* the obligation to build a viable economy.
- The need to address the needs of victims of past abuse *and* to recognise that it is in the interest of victims for perpetrators to be reintegrated into society.

The short essays included in the pages that follow address some of the key terms, questions and dynamics of justice and reconciliation. Far from the last word, they are about means and ends, the ways in which societies can begin the work of transition, and the successes and pitfalls that frequently attend radical social and political change. In all cases, the essays are intended for citizens and activists who want to know more about the contemporary debate on transitional justice and the dynamics of reconciliation, and for those who want to know more in a practical way.

What is restorative justice? What are the different ways of defining and pursuing reconciliation? When is amnesty important and when are prosecutions crucial for those guilty of gross violations of human rights? What are some of the tasks that appear after the old order has been disbanded? Here, we offer some direct replies to these questions, along with lists of resources for those who wish to pursue their investigations further.

Together, these essays indicate that sustainable political reconciliation in pursuit of an inclusive understanding of justice is indeed a difficult puzzle. It is our hope that the offerings here will help clarify something of its picture and contribute to the kinds of dialogue that can help contribute to the work of placing at least some of the puzzle's pieces.

RECONCILIATION

SECTION 1

1 Reconciliation

Charles Villa-Vicencio

Justice and reconciliation are inherently and inextricably linked. In
societies emerging from violent conflict, political reconciliation is not
a romantic or utopian ideal. It is often the only *realistic* alternative
to enduring and escalating violence, and a vital means of building
a society based on the rule of law and social reconstruction.

It is unrealistic to ask victims and survivors of gross violations
of human rights to reconcile in the absence of justice. It is, at the
same time, necessary to broaden the understanding of justice to
include realistic options for the building of civic trust, the promotion
of a human rights culture and the pursuit of economic transformation.
Realistic programmes of reconciliation suggest ways of getting there.
They are about a holistic understanding of justice.

Reconciliation is not easy. Some regard reconciliation or restoration
as meaningless for the simple reason that they simply have no
tangible memory of peace – nothing to restore or return. For many,
the reality of suffering is still too raw to contemplate the possibility
of reconciliation, while others simply resolve never to reconcile. In
the wake of conflict, victims and survivors frequently believe that
justice must come before reconciliation.

Different kinds of conflict require different forms and ways of
reconciliation. At individual and interpersonal levels, reconciliation
may require the healing of deep psychological and emotional wounds.
Political reconciliation demands a different focus, one that involves

less forgiveness than a desire and opportunity for sustained and meaningful interaction. It is unlikely that any person or group will ever be deeply reconciled with everyone else in society. Thus, reconciliation does not provide an immediate or quick solution to the problems facing the nation, and involves a willingness to work together with one's enemies and adversaries in the common pursuit of a solution that is not yet in hand. Reconciliation holds the beginning of civic trust, a willingness to talk, a capacity to listen and a readiness to take cautious risks. It regards justice as an essential ingredient to any settlement, while recognising that there are different ways of achieving and understanding justice.

STRIVING FOR A PROCESS AND A GOAL

Political reconciliation is a beginning. It involves a process and it is something that strives towards a goal. Rarely linear, its process is uneven and may involve lapses into counterproductive, if not violent ways, of redressing conflict. As such, reconciliation requires restraint, generosity of spirit, empathy and perseverance. At the same time, this difficult task is sustained and energised by concrete goals, and a shared vision of what can and might yet be accomplished.

Political reconciliation is the art of turning the possible into the real and is driven by a desire to stretch the limits of what seems possible at a given time. Reconciliation strives to go beyond the normal, recognising that a failure to set in motion programmes to address such sources of conflict which include the demand for retribution, acknowledgement, reparations, poverty relief and access to land will result in little more than delayed violence. Political reconciliation involves taking the first steps to achieve the higher goal of sustainable peace. In the words of a Dinka elder, reflecting on the Sudanese conflict, 'reconciliation begins by agreeing to sit under the same tree with your enemy, to find a way of addressing the causes of the conflict.' This is a process that prioritises dialogue and understanding.

At a deeper level, reconciliation suggests that people are incomplete to the extent that they are alienated from one another. While strategic concerns and political impasse motivate conflict resolution, peace-making and the need for co-existence, the will to live a fulfilled life is often a crucial motive for reconciliation. To recognise the deeper human impulse to know peace is to create the kind of future that enables people to engage one another in the construction of a society that includes others on the basis of human dignity, mutual respect and social justice. Grounded in the African philosophy of *Ubuntu*, reconciliation creates a context for learning to live together.

A MODEST CONCEPT

Political reconciliation is necessarily a modest concept. When moral demands are too high, social momentum suffers. Abstract definitions of reconciliation that involve romanticised notions of repentance, forgiveness and restitution are often politically unhelpful. The *Oxford Concise Dictionary* provides a useful definition of the process and suggests that it involves 'a satisfactory way of dealing with opposing facts and ideas'. It is a concept that has its root in the Latin word *Concilium*, a term that described how antagonists would meet in council to settle their disputes – a first and a necessary step in the reconciling process. For the early Greeks, reconciliation meant finding those words that could 'turn enmity into friendship'.

Niggling debates about what is and is not required for reconciliation to happen are enough to persuade most people that precise definitions and formulas for reconciliation often do more harm than good. Reconciliation defies reduction to a neat set of rules. It is more than a theory and there are no simple 'how to' steps involved. It includes serendipity, imagination, risk and the exploration of what it means 'to start again'. It involves grace. 'It is more than what any one of us can bring to the table. It is something that emerges out of sitting at the table,' suggested a Mozambican woman involved in peace-making between the Front for the Liberation of Mozambique (FRELIMO) and the Mozambican National Resistance Movement (RENAMO). 'It is a gift that comes from the spirit of the ancestors.' It is a celebration of the human spirit.

SOME BENCHMARKS

Reconciliation strives to transcend the logic of what seems possible while ensuring that the crossbar is never so high that people shy away from it. In simple terms, the practice of reconciliation involves addressing the ways and means of building relations. Across neighbourhoods, communities and the nation, this engagement often has a discernable pattern. The benchmarks that follow are about seeking to sit under the same tree, and the ways in which some of the concerns that have the capacity to destroy a nation can be addressed.

Reconciliation does not necessarily involve forgiveness.
Political reconciliation is not dependent on the kind of intimacy
that religious and some forms of individual reconciliation
may demand. Rather, statecraft and politics require peaceful
co-existence. In deeply divided societies, reconciliation needs
to promote mutual understanding and collective action.
Forgiveness may come later, after the creation of confidence
and the building of trust.

Reconciliation interrupts an established pattern of events.
At the lowest level, it may mean an agreement to stop killing one
another – to simply walk by on the other side of the street.
Although an improvement on violence, this sense of reconciliation
is insufficient if it does not interrupt cycles of conflict and turn
silent forms of tolerance toward interactions that allow enemies to
consider what they might have in common, and how these might
be used to invent new ways of existing together.

Reconciliation is a process.
Reconciliation is often as painful as it is costly and it often requires
moral compromise. It involves negotiating with one's memory,
and deciding which of those memories is to have the last word.
At times, it necessitates breaking ranks with one's allies. It is not
for the faint-hearted or easily defeated and clearly some have no
obvious desire to go in search of it at all, making even the thought
of reconciliation a burdensome endeavour.

In short, reconciliation cannot be imposed. It takes time. When
past battles are carried from one generation to another, a lifetime
may not be long enough. The stories of the former Yugoslavia
and Northern Ireland illustrate this problem. Still, the art of
reconciliation has much to do with making time, with seizing those
moments that hold the opportunity to find the common ground
needed to rebuild local community and promote nation-building.

Reconciliation is about talking.
Above all, reconciliation is about communication – careful listening
and deep conversation at every level of society. It involves a national,
inclusive conversation. It is about creating space for individuals and
communities to hear one another, beginning the difficult work of
understanding. While this talk is sometimes argumentative and
characterised by disagreement, it is equally an alternative to violence
and a way to generate solutions to seemingly intractable problems.

Reconciliation requires time and space for mourning, anger and hurt, as well as for healing.

Indeed, the former is often part of the latter. The culture of reconciliation in South Africa, symbolised in the magnanimity of the lives of former President Mandela and Archbishop Tutu, does not always make it easy for some to mourn with the emotion that they may demand or need. Reconciliation requires that there be room for mourning and the release of anger in ways that allow victims to heal and which afford the nation a chance to productively recognise and redress the wounds of the past.

Reconciliation entails understanding.

Understanding does not necessarily lead to reconciliation. Still, when the story of a perpetrator is thoughtfully and truthfully told, empathetically heard and deeply understood, it can soften the perception that the victim, survivor or observer has of the perpetrator. This sort of understanding opens space for a new kind of interaction between adversaries. Politically and morally, the issue is how to promote both remembrance and mutual understanding. Reconciliation involves neither reducing evil to a level where it is condoned nor remembering it in a manner that rekindles the desire for revenge.

Reconciliation involves an acknowledgment of truth.

Acknowledgment of what happened is sometimes more important than knowledge of the facts involved. Although not all who suffered necessarily need a formal apology in order to let go of past conflicts, research into the South African Truth and Reconciliation Commission (TRC) amnesty process shows that acceptance of the outcome increases significantly when the victim or family of the victims receives acknowledgement and a legitimate apology.

Reconciliation is about memory.

It is sometimes suggested that a new order cannot be served by dwelling on a painful past. The problem is that there is no zero hour for starting anew. History lives on, shapes the present and will threaten the future. Unspoken memory cries out to be heard. It needs to be dealt with, not only to uncover the truth about the past, but also as a way of dealing with the future. Many of the stories victims told to the TRC had less to do with what actually happened, and more to do with the impact of what happened on the present and future lives of victims.

Reconciliation is about pursuing justice.

There can be no lasting reconciliation without justice, which in many instances includes the understandable demand by some for retribution and restitution. A comprehensive notion of justice cannot, however, be realised or sustained without the embedded patterns of conflict being dealt with. Political reconciliation is about finding ways of dealing with this tension as a basis for ensuring that peace and justice are both realised and sustained.

Reconciliation includes reparations.

The debate on the nature and scope of reparations for victims of gross violations of human rights will persist. To exclude socio-economic justice from the process of reconciliation is to endanger the prospects of democratic consolidation. At its best, the objective of reparations is to integrate the objective and the subjective, to transcend both the material and emotional divides of the past. It is about the creation of a different kind of society.

It's about survival.

Reconciliation will remain a difficult concept, a challenge that taxes our capacity for understanding and will demand new ways of feeling and interacting. However, this does not mean that the need for reconciliation will go away anytime soon.

Reconciliation is a long process: one that takes time and involves dealing with the past. It is work that entails mourning, listening, understanding, healing, acknowledgement and reparations. It is a beginning and a basis for creating a new way of living.

Reconciliation begins when people who are at odds with one another learn to deal with conflicts in a humane manner. This is the hope located at the heart of reconciliation: the idea that being human involves a process of engagement between strangers and adversaries; an interaction that can serve as a space within which to deal creatively with issues (material and emotional) that can make us less than human. It is a space within which to deal with demands for justice in a comprehensive and integrated way.

Against the potential for self and mutual destruction, reconciliation requires that individuals think and work beyond 'me and my future', to embrace a concern for 'we and our future'. In this way, reconciliation is a form of political realism rather than interpersonal forgiveness. It is about surviving and growing together. The alternative is further polarisation, the escalation of violence and an intensification of human suffering.

FURTHER READING:

Raymond G Helmic and Rodney L Petersen, eds, *Forgiveness and Reconciliation: Religious, Public Policy and Conflict Transformation*. (Radnor, PA: Templeton Foundation Press, 2001).

Martha Minow, *Between Vengeance and Forgiveness: Facing History After Genocide and Mass Violence*. (Boston: Beacon Books, 1998).

Donald Shriver, *An Ethic for Enemies: Forgiveness in Politics*. (New York and Oxford: Oxford University Press, 1995).

Desmond Tutu, *No Future Without Forgiveness*. (Canada: Rider, 1999).

2   Ubuntu

Dani W Nabudere

As an African notion, *ubuntu* is about the essence of being human. It is part of the gift that Africans give to the world. It is expressed in the Zulu maxim, 'a person is a person through other persons'. Archbishop Desmond Tutu speaks of it as 'humanness' and as the philosophy of a shared humanity in which we define ourselves through our relations with other people: 'my humanity is caught up, is inextricably bound up in yours. I am human because I belong, I participate, I share. What dehumanises you inexorably dehumanises me.'

The solitary individual is a contradiction in terms. To work for the common good is to enable your humanity to come into its own. *Ubuntu* embraces hospitality, caring about others and a willingness to go that extra mile for the sake of others. It involves the individual being an individual in community, and belonging within that social, moral and political framework. *Ubuntu* thus provides a philosophical basis for reconciliation in the aftermath of violent conflict.

Ubuntu philosophy, in its different settings, can be seen as an integral part of African people's struggle to survive and exist in human community in the midst of colonialism, apartheid and other forms of exploitation. It has underpinned attempts to settle disputes and conflicts at different levels on the continent, and is central to the ideas of community and political reconciliation. The search for an African philosophical explanation of the experience gained under the Truth and Reconciliation Commission (TRC) has also added momentum to this interest in the emergence of this philosophy. More recently, discussions about *ubuntu* have gained momentum amidst political developments in South Africa encapsulated by President Thabo Mbeki's call for an 'African Renaissance'. This testifies to the dynamism and vibrancy of this philosophy in whatever African linguistic expression it may take place.

It does not, of course, follow that all Africans propagate, practise or are consciously aware of the philosophy any more than any other philosophy of life is practiced or propagated by those who live under its influence. Indeed, some who are aware of it dismiss it as a post-colonial utopian invention and/or a prophetic illusion crafted by African political elites in the age of globalisation. Some of the critics even question the philosophy on the grounds that, at best, it is a Bantu philosophy not related to the ways of life and outlook of other 'tribal' groupings of Africa. On the other hand, many scholars observe that *ubuntu* is part of the worldview of Africans in most parts of the continent, stretching from the Nubian Desert in the Sudan to the Cape of Good Hope, and from Senegal to Zanzibar.

Amidst this debate, a view is increasingly emerging that, while Africa lagged behind Europe technologically and economically, it was ahead of Europe in terms of its social and political philosophies and systems. These systems, which revolved around communal relationships, explain the respect for human values and the recognition of human worth that is the basis of *ubuntu*, as well as the social structures that provide a sense of living together that European philosophic systems often fail to promote.

UBUNTU AS AN AFRICAN PHILOSOPHY

In this context, the rejuvenation of the philosophy of *ubuntu* is important, both for its contribution to political reconciliation and for the ways in which it provides Africans with a sense of self-identity, self-respect and a basis for social reconstruction. It enables Africans to deal with conflict in a positive manner by drawing on the humanistic values handed down to them through their history. Politically and philosophically, Africans can make a unique contribution of these values to the quest for peaceful co-existence in the world.

Ubuntu, African scholars have increasingly observed, forms the basis of the African philosophy of being. *Ubuntu* is the root of the African tree of knowledge, in which *ubu*, evokes the idea of unfolding towards 'being in general' and *ntu* denotes 'being human'. Together, the words suggest the wholeness and oneness of all life, the location of individual humanness within the larger whole. *Ubuntu* is thus linked to *umuntu*, or the individual person in community with others. As an individual living in relation to others, *umuntu* is the creator of politics, religion and law, and the maker of worlds that are constantly emerging and constantly changing. Through these creative activities, *umuntu* gains experience, knowledge and a philosophy of life based on truth. An African philosophy of life and reflection of lived historical experience, *ubuntu* is more than a philosophical abstraction. This is where African philosophy differs from most western analytical philosophies.

In his or her existence and being, *umuntu* strives to create conditions for existence with other beings. A Bantu proverb puts it this way: '*Umuntu* ngumuntu ngabantu', which literally means 'a person is a person through other persons.' *Ubuntu* is therefore about 'being with others'. The expression is found in many other African languages, including Sotho: 'motho ke motho ka batho'. To achieve this togetherness, reconciliation with others is motivated and driven by the will and need 'to be', by being truly one's self, a condition that is necessarily achieved through relations forged with others.

UBUNTU, METAPHYSICS AND RELIGION

Ubuntu is deeply metaphysical, particularly in response to conflict and the ways in which reconciliation is made possible. Their long history of conflict makes African people, like many others who have suffered entrenched periods of conflict, acutely aware of uncertainty and death. Traditionally, for most Africans, death does not mean the disappearance of the dead. The dead are rather understood to continue in a spirit form and as such are recognised as the 'living-dead' or ancestors. According to *ubuntu* philosophy, the ancestors reveal their ongoing presence through the lives of the living. Specifically, ancestors can, when called upon, intercede and advise the living on what needs to be done. Such intercession forms a crucial part of reconciliation rituals.

In addition to the ancestors, there are also the 'un-born', who are understood as existing in the future. As such, the living are required to ensure that the unborn are brought into the world and that the world is prepared to receive them, in much the same way that they are required to remember those that lived before them. Differently stated, as the individual is related to the community, so too is the present age linked to the past and to the future.

Life is thus seen to embrace the un-born, the living and the living-dead. It is a world of beings both visible and invisible, in which it is possible for the living to engage with the unknown in ways that have a direct influence on their own being, behaviour and obligations. These invisible forces represent a set of African explanations for life that cannot easily be explained in terms of Western rationality. Conflict is understood as an integral part of uncertainty in human existence, and supernatural beings, as part of that unexplained world, have a privileged understanding of it. They represent historical perspective and future needs.

Ubuntu also allows for religious diversity. Many Africans believe in one God, while others believe in a variety of gods and spirits. Christianity and Islam have, of course, come to influence African spirituality, but this has not done away with African traditional religious beliefs. The result is that many African Christians and Muslims today continue to practise African religions in what is normally called African Christianity, Islam in Africa and/or syncretism. Rather than seeing religions as competing, Africans are often able to straddle different belief systems, combining them into a single one.

Ubuntu philosophy involves a deep respect for all people's religious beliefs and practices. This respect opens space in African thinking for a mix of practices in which reconciliation develops a fuller meaning than it does in most religions; not least in its respect for the other, without requiring conversion or assimilation. It reaches towards a synthesis beyond the antithesis, reflected in the recollections of veteran anti-apartheid activist, Ruth Mompati:

> I came from a home where no contradiction was seen between the Church and traditional rituals. Both religions were seen to affirm the same ends in life, the worship of God and the affirmation of decent, moral living. I grew up with a religion that stressed the importance of being a warm human being, hospitable, generous, concerned with the welfare of others and dedicated to caring for outcasts, the weak and the desolate.

UBUNTU, POLITICS AND LAW

With *ubuntu*, reconciliation is based on a thoroughly African understanding of politics and law. People make politics and law, specifically seeking the adherence of all community members. African law is a living law, based on a recognition of the continuity and wholeness of life, embracing the living, the living-dead and the unborn. It involves the present, the past and the future. Law, at best, is a combination of rules of behaviour, which are embodied in the flow of daily life. There is no individual above the law. An act of reconciliation is therefore understood to have the full force of African legal and political philosophy behind it; recognising that law and politics is about engagement, negotiation and agreement. As such, reconciliation necessarily involves dealing with the tough issues that divide people and nations. Similarly, in *ubuntu* political philosophy, royal power is expected to spring from the people, who are the true sovereign.

Clearly, African post-colonial leadership is frequently not reflective of *ubuntu* rule, being guilty of despotic and authoritarian behaviour. It follows that if the African Renaissance is to succeed, it must lead to a cessation of repressive rule and social exclusion. It must initiate a politics of inclusiveness and human security for all. In short, the African Renaissance must lead to power being returned to the people, a development that appears to require a concerted return to *ubuntu* and its direct connection to reconciliation. Herein lies the philosophy and spiritual energy that this continent so desperately needs.

UBUNTU AND RECONCILIATION

Reconciliation as a philosophy and practice is an essential element in most human relationships. The South African Truth and Reconciliation Commission (TRC) has become a symbol of hope around the world for its attempt to bring about peace and political reconciliation between widely divergent groups. It sought to promote accountability, restoration and reconciliation. The extent of its success is often attributed to the Christian nature of South African society. It, at the same time, needs to be recognised that the process can (and must) also be understood in terms of *ubuntu*.

The TRC has specifically been criticised by some for not evoking sufficient confession, remorse or repentance from perpetrators. Such religious experiences, it is argued, are necessary for the renewal of any society. It also needs to be acknowledged that for the divisive past to be transformed, the common humanity of former enemies needs to be acknowledged as a basis for drawing all those involved in the conflict into a common future. Any viable notion of reconciliation, whatever its religious or philosophical grounding, understands this. *Ubuntu* offers a realistic and important contribution to this process, reflected in the response of Cynthia Ngewu at the TRC hearings to the killer of her son: 'If reconciliation means this perpetrator, this man who killed Christopher Piet, if it means he becomes human again, so that I, so that all of us, get our humanity back, then I agree, then I support it all.'

CONCLUSION

Reconciliation under the African philosophy of *ubuntu* offers different approaches to overcoming and transforming conflicts of different kinds at different levels. Aiming towards sustained peace, it has an important role to play in managing Africa's conflicts. At first, reconciliation involves a few people, but eventually it leads to the reorientation of the relations between the combatants to include a wider community. Even critics of *ubuntu* agree that where conflict recurs, the act of reconciliation constitutes a reordering of relations in which the central idea of conflict transformation is implied. *Ubuntu* therefore contains an effective basis for conflict management in which, to quote Wim van Binsbergen, 'the secret of the village headman's skill who, while lacking all formal sanctions, yet through the imaginative power of reconciliation, manages to safeguard the conflicting interests of the members of his community, without destroying any of them.'

It follows that reconciliation under the *ubuntu* philosophy can be invoked to deal with conflicts in other countries, including seemingly intractable international conflicts. 'An eye for an eye' and 'a tooth for a tooth' is the kind of philosophy that is bound to lead to everyone involved in the conflict to become blind and toothless! The global community of the 21st century can draw inspiration from excavating the depths of African philosophy for the benefit of all humanity. In this way, it may be possible for Africa to claim the 21st century to be an African century and the African Renaissance to be a humanising experience for all humanity.

MPATAPO: 'Knot of pacification/reconciliation'. A symbol of reconciliation, peace-making and pacification, the Mpatapo, emanating from the Andikra religion of West Africa, represents the bond or knot that binds parties in a dispute to a peaceful, harmonious reconciliation.

FURTHER READING:

R B G Choudree, Traditions of Conflict Resolution in Africa.
  African Journal on Conflict Resolution, 1 (1999). Reprinted at:
http://www.accord.org.za/ajcr/1999–1/accordr_v1_n1_a2.pdf
  [Accessed 20 October 2004].
Jannie Malan, *Conflict Resolution Wisdom from Africa*.
  (Durban: Accord, 1997).
Mogobe B Ramose, *African Philosophy through Ubuntu*.
  (Harare: Mond Books, 1999).
Wim van Binsbergen, 'Ubuntu and the Globalisation of Southern
  African Thought and Society'. *Quest*, 15 (2001).

16

3   Peace Processes

John Darby

Nations containing more than one ethnic or national group – that is to say, all nations – are likely to experience some level of ethnic conflict. If they are functioning societies, their differences will be managed relatively successfully through state institutions, including: politics, the courts and civil society. If not, they are likely to experience some level of violence.

If plural societies were charted on a graph according to how effectively they function, the pattern might be presented as an ascending line. At the bottom of the line are peacefully regulated multi-cultural societies with little or no violence, such as Switzerland, Canada and Australasia. All of these have experienced ethnic tensions, and sometimes violence, in the past and may experience it again in the future. Moving along the ascending line, a large number of communities suffer relatively low levels of ethnic violence, including (in the present or recent past) the Basque Country and Northern Ireland. At the top of the graph are societies in which the violence has spiralled out of control, such as experienced in Bosnia, Rwanda and Burundi. These are often characterised by open warfare by organised armies.

Some individual societies have completed the full course more than once, while others oscillate around one point over prolonged periods. It is sometimes possible, especially during early phases of ethnic violence, to address grievances through the introduction of appropriate policies, and to initiate or strengthen progress towards a more peaceful accommodation. It is also possible for low-violence ethnic conflicts to be suppressed temporarily rather than returning to the controlled but unresolved state from which they sprang. If ethnic grievances are not addressed rapidly, they tend to accelerate along the line of grievance toward violence. When this happens, it becomes difficult to return to the fundamental causes of the conflict, and the priority may shift to reducing the casualties from planning for a post-war settlement.

Since the early 1990s, many divided societies have attempted to forestall this escalatory tendency, or to pick up the pieces after it, by embarking on a peace process. There were, of course, many attempts to resolve conflicts before that time, but the collapse of a superpower system ushered in a new approach to peace-making. Its characteristics were clear. It was less likely to involve the United Nations (UN), except in catastrophes like in the former Yugoslavia. It was more likely to be generated and driven by the parties in conflict, often with significant external encouragement and support, as in South Africa and Northern Ireland. As a result, new approaches to negotiation emerged. The 'new' processes were highly imitative, and negotiators were eager to 'borrow' from other contemporary (rather than historical) processes.

Since 1990, there have been more than 30 major settlements and dozens of partial ones. In 2004 alone, there have been three new comprehensive peace agreements, with varying degrees of stability, in Burundi, the Democratic Republic of the Congo and Angola. So there has been a formidable increase in our knowledge about recent and contemporary peace processes. What can one say in general about them? What guidance can they offer for negotiators? Where do we stand?

SIX PROPOSITIONS

In 2000, Roger MacGinty and I presented a series of eight propositions, based on a study of five peace processes conducted between 1996 and 2000. All these processes, of course, are singular. It is not possible to understand a peace process without knowing about a country's particular history, social relationships and politics. The propositions were drawn up at a time when there was optimism, if not about all the processes themselves, about the new approaches to peace-making that were evolving within them. The optimism has been somewhat tempered by experience. In light of research carried out in the short intervening period, six of the propositions are here presented in a revised and modified form. They come with a healthy

warning. Some of them may seem morally distasteful. These
are based on empirical observations, not moral aspirations.

Proposition 1

Most ceasefires collapse in the first few months. The survivors
are likely to deliver some level of success.

If a peace process survives its initial nervousness, it tends to
strengthen. Sometimes it is reinforced by internal pressure from
public opinion, as it so happened in South Africa when the process
faltered in 1992. This dynamic does not mean that the negotiators
have become friends. From the start of the Northern Ireland
process in 1994 until well after the Good Friday Agreement in 1998,
Unionists refused even to speak directly to members of Sinn Féin.
Thus, it is sufficient that opponents define a common problem
and attempt to negotiate an accommodation.

The dynamic of achieving this position locks those involved
in negotiation in an uncomfortable embrace. The participants
become more attracted to the positive rewards of a historic
breakthrough. It becomes increasingly difficult for any of them
to contemplate a return to the earlier violence. Failure to make
progress would rule out another initiative for the foreseeable
future. It would also probably mean the end of their political
careers and, sometimes, threaten their lives.

In addition, working relationships develop between the negotiators
as they concentrate on the practical minutiae of negotiations and
become better acquainted with the boundaries within which their
opponents operate. These benefits are far from guaranteed. They
depend on maintaining forward momentum. Persistent stalemates
may confirm initial suspicions and lead to a strengthening of the
internal cohesion of competing parties, and an erosion of the
common ground identified during negotiations; as happened
within both the Israeli and Palestinian communities in late 2000.

Generally speaking, the further the process develops, the
stronger its shock-absorbent facility and the greater its ability to
withstand the inevitable atrocities designed to undermine it. The
policy implication is to focus economic and political support on
the initial stages of the process.

Proposition 2

A lasting agreement is impossible unless it actively involves
those with the power to bring it down by violence.

Is it possible to make a settlement without including parties with militant associations? Many peace processes were sparked by the decision to include militants in negotiations. The settlement in South Africa started with the release of Nelson Mandela and African National Congress (ANC) prisoners in 1990. In Northern Ireland, there were seven unsuccessful attempts to reach agreement through negotiation between constitutional politicians, until the inclusion of Sinn Féin and the loyalist parties led to the Good Friday Agreement. Recent developments in peace processes reinforce this conclusion. It is difficult to think of a situation where serious ethnic violence was terminated without either unacceptable repression or the involvement of those perpetrating the violence. The failure of the Colombian government's approach to the Revolutionary Armed Forces of Columbia (FARC) in 1998 is a warning that the involvement of militants in talks is a necessary condition, but not a sufficient one, for success.

Total inclusion is never possible. There are always zealots who will not compromise, so the demand for inclusive talks is always a qualified one. Just as the principle of 'sufficient consensus' was adopted in South Africa in recognition of the impossibility of progress if all participants had veto powers, a principle of 'sufficient inclusion' may be applied to militant organisations. This does not mean the inclusion of all parties using or threatening to use violence. The principle of 'sufficient inclusion' is that a peace process includes both all the actors who represent a significant proportion of their community, and all the actors who have the ability to destroy an agreement. The two groups are often coterminous.

Proposition 3

Spoiler groups can only be neutralised with the active involvement of ex-militants.

Agreement by violent groups to negotiate is never unanimous. It often leads to the formation of splinter groups determined to continue the armed struggle. If they later enter the process, additional breakaway spoilers may emerge. The actions of spoilers move increasingly towards the margins during and after the process of peace negotiations. This traffic raises the question of how spoiler violence will be tackled by a coalition government including former militants.

At some point during the process, when all the splinter groups likely to join the process have done so, two rumps may remain – mavericks that are engaged in crime for personal advantage and ideological zealots. They pose different problems. It is relatively straightforward

to criminalise the former and to confront them through a reformed police force and justice system acceptable across the community. It is much more difficult for ex-militants to turn against groups who share their general orientation, but have refused to buy into the peace process.

Proposition 4

During peace negotiations the primary function of leaders is to deliver their own people. Assisting their opponents in the process is secondary.

Peace accords are negotiated by power holders and power seekers, who must then persuade their followers to endorse it through an election or referendum. Power holders represent those (usually, but not always, the state) who have traditionally controlled the reins of government. The power seekers want to alter the prevailing political, economic, legal and cultural arrangements, often by force. The work needed to prepare their followers for compromise usually starts many years before it becomes public.

The transitional problems facing both power holders and power seekers are superficially similar. In both cases, extremist rather than moderate leaders are more likely to deliver suspicious followers. Reluctant converts, like Buthelezi and Viljoen in South Africa, are more convincing and trusted by the extremes. At this point the similarity ends. The power holders – usually the state – enter into negotiations because they recognise the inevitability of change before their followers do; their main difficulty is to convince their supporters that the resulting changes are minimal. The power seekers – usually militant leaders – get into negotiation because they recognise the advantages of negotiation before their followers do; their main difficulty is to convince their supporters that the negotiations are achieving major concessions. If the process moves too slowly, it hurts the power seekers. If it moves too speedily, it hurts the power holders.

Proposition 5

Members of the security forces and paramilitary groups must be integrated into normal society if a peace agreement is to stick. A natural consequence is that peace accords need to address the needs of victims of violence.

Prudence demands that those who were engaged in the war must be provided with jobs and training. The ending of violence leaves an inheritance of high risk. The shrinkage of the security industry – army, police, prison officers and private security guards – brings on to the unemployment register people skilled in the use of arms. A similar risk of redundancy faces those militants whose lives have been devoted to armed resistance. Their speedy return to civil society is essential, less because they deserve a reward than because they have the means to destabilise the peace process.

If there is the need to re-integrate ex-militants and members of the security forces into society, there is also the need to anticipate society's response to the provision of preferential treatment for people convicted of murder, bombings and mutilations. In the interests of equity, but also in order to manage the peace process successfully, any moves to re-integrate militants into society must be balanced by recognition of the needs of their bereaved and the wounded. Each society must find a form appropriate to its traditions and circumstances.

Proposition 6

A peace process does not end with a peace accord.

There are no rules about the best time to reach formal agreement during a peace process. The agreements in Northern Ireland and Israel were only made possible by postponing some contentious issues for later resolution, leaving enormous trip wires to traverse in the post-accord period. Even in South Africa, where a remarkably broad range of agreements had been agreed before the 1994 elections, the issues of truth and reconciliation lingered well into the future.

If negotiators wait until all major issues have been resolved, the process may collapse from mutual distrust or violence before they reach a conclusion. If they defer complex and divisive issues for later resolution, it will be more difficult to contain negotiations as mutual fears and suspicions flourish among the uncertainty. In either case, post-settlement euphoria may be followed by post-agreement disillusionment. If so, the all-important momentum may be lost.

It is increasingly evident that many peace processes fail after apparent agreement has been reached through an accord. The causes and dynamics are varied and under-studied, but some guidelines are evident. Parties may wish to re-negotiate some provisions in an agreement that they cannot sell to their supporters. Public expectations, initially raised by any agreement, are often dashed by an inability to implement them, compounding the problems during negotiations with added distrust. The problems and challenges which emerge after an accord are new, so there are fewer guidelines available for tackling them. They are likely to assume a more urgent research priority in coming years.

CHANGING PATTERNS IN PEACE-MAKING

Even in the last quarter century, approaches to conflict between ethno-nationalist groups have undergone systemic changes. During the 1980s, the superpowers still claimed major responsibility for maintaining order. The Soviet Union discouraged dissention in Yugoslavia and Czechoslovakia, the United States in Latin America. During the 1990s, this was supplemented and occasionally replaced by the shift towards internal negotiations already described.

Are we currently witnessing another significant change? Certainly the war against terrorism is having a significant effect on internal conflicts, both on governments and on their opponents. Some states have taken advantage of the war against terrorism to clamp down on internal dissidents and move towards a tougher security approach. This has been particularly marked in states with Muslim minorities like Israel and the Philippines, but has also been evident in other states with dissident militants such as Nepal and Spain. The militants have also been affected. Tougher security approaches have boosted resistance struggles in many Muslim countries, including Iraq, the Philippines and Palestine. Paradoxically, other armed militants, especially those depending on diaspora support, such as dissident Irish republican groups and the Tamil Tigers, have been forced to limit their campaigns. So the effect has been somewhat contradictory.

It is too early to judge whether these are permanent changes in the world of peace-making, but it raises two significant questions. Are we witnessing the end of the peace process, as developed since the 1990s? If so, what will replace it?

FURTHER READING:

Chester A Crocker, Fen O Hampson and Pamela Aall, eds, *Herding Cats: Multiparty Mediation in a Complex World.* (Washington DC: United States Institute of Peace Press, 1999).

John Darby, *The Effects of Violence on Peace Processes.* (Washington, DC: United States Institute of Peace Press, 2001).

John Darby and Roger MacGinty, eds, *Contemporary Peace Making.* (London and New York: Palgrave-Macmillan, 2003).

Hugh Miall, Oliver Ramsbotham and Tom Woodhouse. *Contemporary Conflict Resolution.* (London: Macmillan, 1998).

S J Stedman, D Rothchild and E M Cousens, eds, *Ending Civil Wars: The Implementation of Peace Agreements.* (Boulder, Colorado: Lynne Rienner, 2002).

I W Zartman, ed., *Elusive Peace: Negotiating an End to Civil Wars.* (Washington, DC: Brookings Institution, 1995).

4   Reparation

Erik Doxtader

Reparations both compensate and promise. As a marker of (in)justice, they are also a source of controversy. In the wake of systemic political violence, atrocity and gross violations of human rights, reparation is a transitional instrument that acknowledges the offenses of the past and provides a basis for building a new future. The difficulty, however, is that reparations are never enough. The past cannot be undone, lost potential can never be fully recovered and the reparative gesture is inevitably partial. In the midst of transition, the call for reparations gives rise to difficult questions: Who deserves and requires reparation? In what form? For how long? To what end?

While the term 'reparation' has ancient roots, its formal role in the history of conflict resolution is a modern phenomenon. In ancient times, the word conveyed a sense of return, an undoing or a turning back of the clock in the name of restoring individuals and communities to a prior condition. Linked closely to restitution, reparation is often considered to involve an act of law, an official recognition and redress of a basic harm or injustice. In this sense, reparation is a form and moment of remembrance. It names an injustice, acknowledges its harm (often through appeal to legal precedent) and provides a means for its redress. As such, some kinds of reparation may appear to have a retributive quality insofar as those responsible for the harm caused are called to provide victims with compensation.

In other cases, however, reparation operates as an alternative to retribution, particularly in situations where reparation functions as a counterpart to amnesty, and when a new government undertakes to repair the damage done by its predecessor. In any event, reparation focuses attention on how the past bears on the present and what actions are needed to move to the future. This is a difficult process, especially as it forces victims and perpetrators to confront the hidden and often contentious truth of history. Reparation depends on reaching agreements about what harm has been done and how it is best redressed.

Reparations cannot proceed by formula, nor do they have a fixed form. Their restorative power is contingent on the kind of conflict that has been waged, the perceptions of those who have suffered and the political realities of a negotiated settlement. Most often, reparation is defined in material terms. Money, reconstruction programmes, physical and psychological health benefits, educational opportunities and land can all have a reparative function, allowing the dispossessed to regain their footing and begin again. In some cases, these grants are made to individual victims or their surviving family members. In others, communal or social reparation may be more appropriate in redressing legacies of material inequality. Necessarily, these resources have a symbolic quality and do not actually return victims and communities to a prior state of affairs so much as acknowledge that their future livelihood depends on directed and sustained support. Moreover, many victims of gross human rights violations may be less interested in material compensation than in memorials that unearth and explain the truth of the past, and set the stage for debate about how to prevent the repetition of violence and subjugation. Oral histories, spaces for community remembrance, museums, monuments and the (re)naming of public facilities can all serve reparative ends.

REPARATION AND INTERNATIONAL LAW

The duty to make reparations in the wake of gross human rights violations is both clearly established and rendered ambiguous by the terms of international law. In 1928, for instance, the Permanent Court of International Justice argued that reparation was an inviolable rule of law and that it 'must, as far as possible, wipe out all the consequences of the illegal act and re-establish the situation which would, in all probability, have existed if that act had not been committed.' However, as one commentator has noted, there is today 'no general rule of customary international law to the effect that any grave violation of human rights creates an individual reparation claim under international law.' In short, international law holds open the gap between the desired ends and available means of reparation. Sometimes, international tribunals may hold individuals and groups responsible for the payment of reparation. In other cases, it is government that endeavours to redress the wounds of gross human rights violations. There is also a growing body of law suggesting that corporations may be liable for supporting or benefiting from tyrannical regimes.

The legal nature of reparation is complicated further by the fact that international law tends only to recognise the need for reparative measures in response to specific gross violations of human rights. This focus leaves to the side the question of how to understand and redress the wounds inflicted by structural forms of violence such as South African apartheid – a system that subjugated and exploited millions in a manner that does not always translate into actionable legal claims that can be adjudicated in courts. This shortfall is particularly troublesome to the degree that it raises divisive questions about who deserves reparation and what form of compensation is most appropriate. Moreover, many victims of violence and atrocity may not have access to the courts or the resources needed to undertake lengthy and costly prosecutions that may (or may not) culminate in the payment of reparation. Thus, one danger of leaving reparation in a strictly legal context may be that it raises and then frustrates the expectations of victims, while also creating an adversarial environment that leads perpetrators to fear revenge or prompts them to withdraw from delicate transitional structures altogether.

THE RESTORATIVE JUSTICE OF REPARATION

Beyond the edicts of international law, reparations may serve the ends of restorative justice. Here, the concern is less about strict retribution than a concern for the question of how material and symbolic compensation can work to acknowledge the wounds of the past, restore human dignity and create platforms for collective (re)integration and nation-building. On this interpretation, reparation has much to do with the process of transforming a divided society into one that has the capacity to build a sense of common good and collective unity. At the same time, a restorative model of reparation may *hear* better than its legal counterpart to the degree that it offers

victims a chance to express publicly the experience of their suffering
and their perceptions about how it is best redressed in relation to
the present.

In a basic sense, this truth-telling process proceeds from the
assumption that justice demands forms of reparation that both
recover the standing of victims and help restore the social and
political fabric that has been torn by protracted conflict. Reparation
is thus a relational process, an exchange that opens and invites
opportunities for mutual understanding, reintegration and collective
decision-making. As Charles Villa-Vicencio suggests elsewhere in this
publication, reparations involve the negotiation of a 'difficult justice',
a process in which the understandable desire for revenge is
supplanted by a willingness to undertake forms of reconciliation
that use the horrifying truths of the past to build a collective future.

While less formal than court-sponsored reparation, restorative

models do not necessarily proceed in an *ad hoc* manner. They may be supported by truth commissions, human rights bodies and government agencies dedicated to reallocating land and redressing economic inequality. While the work of such transitional structures may blur the difference between reparation and reconstruction, their potential benefit is an ability to better understand the contextual factors that bear on the appropriate form and content of reparation.

When emerging from protracted conflict, deeply divided societies may confront the fact that not all perpetrators can be brought to book, and that such prosecutions both outstrip available resources and risk a dangerous (re)balkanisation. New governments may not have the resources to compensate victims fully and may be unwilling or unable to demand that those who benefited from the previous system pay their due. In such situations, particularly when amnesty has been offered to perpetrators in the name of unearthing hidden histories of violence and securing a minimum level of political stability, the creation of reparation policy involves a delicate negotiation between social, economic and political imperatives.

REPARATION IN SOUTH AFRICA

The South African transition from apartheid demonstrates the difficulty of making reparation policies that balance accountability, victims' rights and political necessity. In 1994, shortly after Nelson Mandela's inauguration, policy-makers began to debate how to fulfil in the Interim Constitution's mandate for an amnesty that would serve the ends of reconciliation, reconstruction and reparation. Concerned that amnesty could not come at the expense of truth or a 'victim-centered' process of healing, the amnesty process was set into the larger work of the Truth and Reconciliation Commission (TRC), a body that was then authorised to hear testimony from victims, compile a register of those who suffered gross violations of human rights and make recommendations to Parliament about the kinds of reparation that would allow the country to move forward in a spirit of 'understanding but not for vengeance, a need for reparation but not for retaliation, a need for *ubuntu* but not for victimisation.'

Coupled with perceptions as to how the amnesty process compromised the ability of victims to seek justice in the courts, the fact that the TRC did not have the power to pay-out or even guarantee reparation motivated a court challenge to the TRC's work. In 1996, South Africa's Constitutional Court appeared to hold that amnesty was constitutionally permissible if victims of apartheid-era violence were provided reparations. While it recognised the 'agonising balancing act' involved in preserving transitional stability and fulfilling the demands of justice, the Court's ruling did not specify what kinds of reparation were required or when they needed to be distributed. This ambiguity led to substantial controversy and significant tension between the TRC and ANC-led government. While the former advocated a timely and extensive reparation package, including multi-year monetary payments to victims, the latter maintained that the distribution of anything more than emergency relief payments would have to wait until the TRC closed its doors and a final list of victims was compiled. Simultaneously, many in government, including President Thabo Mbeki, argued that individual reparation was not always appropriate given larger communal needs, and that the liberation struggle was not waged for monetary compensation.

Only in 2003 did the South African government authorise a one-time reparation payment of R30 000 to those deemed eligible by the TRC. Frustrated by both delay and a sense that they had not received what they were initially promised, victims have expressed dissatisfaction with the process and in some cases sought relief in other courts.

Outside of government, efforts to mobilise reparation packages from business and other communities that benefited from apartheid have met with very little success.

MAKING REPARATION POLICY

Echoed in many other post-conflict situations, the South African case illustrates the difficult questions that attend the creation of reparation policy. An important element of transition and a crucial means of ensuring both historical memory and accountability, the ultimate success of reparations may depend on the ability of young democracies to deal successfully with a complex set of moral, political and pragmatic problems.

Eligibility requirements for reparation need to be designed with due care and through a transparent process. Given finite resources, states cannot pay something to everyone even when restricting reparation to victims of gross human rights violations, which may unfairly exclude a significant number of individuals. Accordingly, meaningful reparation may depend on a careful accounting of the past, the truth of historical suffering and its myriad forms and causes.

The form of reparation must take into account the nature of the crimes involved, the resources of the nation and the expressed needs of victims. Money is important but it is not always the full answer. For instance, one-time payments may not empower those struggling to recover from a long history of inequality; grants of land may require the provision of funds needed to actually begin farming; memorials need to be designed in close consultation with community members.

Legal procedures for reparation need to be clear from the beginning. Truth commissions that promise reparation but lack the authority to fund policy can easily create unrealistic expectations. Governments need to make clear when and how reparation will be provided.

Reparation cannot be left solely to government and its institutions. If it is to serve the ends of restoration and reconciliation, the process of reparation needs to be a social event, one that creates incentives for beneficiaries of the old regime to contribute to the success of the new dispensation. This work is exceedingly difficult, especially if it alienates beneficiaries through declarations of their individual or collective guilt.

Reparation takes time. At the very least, it is a generation's work, an effort that must proceed within local, communal and national contexts.

In the face of a history that will not 'end', reparation requires close attention to the question of how to craft a present for the future. Much more than an ideal to be achieved in some vague time yet to come, its hope for transformation is a call to act right now. The fact that reparation can neither erase history's pain nor fully compensate for its losses is not a reason to conclude that what is past is past or that legacies imply an inevitability which defies correction. But, this is not to say that there are ready-made solutions. Much more than just a set of policy decisions or court judgments, the power of the reparative may reside in an attitude, a willingness to see historical deprivation and inequality as a common problem that demands the struggle for a future in which things can be made otherwise.

FURTHER READING:

M R Rwelamire and G Werle, eds, *Confronting Past Injustices: Approaches to Amnesty, Punishment, Reparation and Restitution in South Africa and Germany.* (Durban: Butterworths, 1996).

Erik Doxtader and Charles Villa-Vicencio, eds, *To Repair the Irreparable: Reparations and Reconstruction in South Africa.* (Cape Town: David Philip, 2004).

South African Truth and Reconciliation Commission, *Final Report*, Volume 7. (Cape Town: 2003).

Wole Soyinka, *The Burden of Memory, The Muse of Forgiveness.* (New York: Oxford University Press, 1999).

5   Restorative Justice

Charles Villa-Vicencio

Restorative justice is at the heart of the transitional justice debate.
It involves a difficult and contested task. It is boldly contextual.
Grounded in the essential principles of the rule of law and human
rights, it prioritises the beneficence of victims and survivors. At the
same time, it recognises that the restoration of perpetrators of past
human rights abuses is in the interest of victims and survivors as well
as society as a whole. The need is, in the words of Ismael Mahomed,
the late South African Constitutional Court Justice, for perpetrators
to 'become active, full and creative members of the new order'. The
need, suggests Mahomed, is for both victims and perpetrators to
cross the historic bridge from the past to the future, not 'with heavy
dragged steps delaying and impeding a rapid and enthusiastic
transition to the new society at the end of the bridge.'

A DIFFICULT JUSTICE

Justice in situations of transition is not self-defining. It is about
what is required and what is possible in a given situation. There
are different kinds of justice: *retributive justice, deterrent justice,
compensatory justice, rehabilitative justice, exonerative justice and
restorative justice*. Each has a time and a place in a given situation
and no one model of justice covers all needs. The balance between
individual, communal and national demands needs constant

attention, while recognising that the different levels of restoration are inherently linked. The one feeds off the other. To integrate the demands of each of these levels is the essence of restorative rule.

A viable society cannot afford to elevate one set of needs to the exclusion or neglect of others, and still have the centre hold. Justice is about enabling a nation, which includes former enemies and adversaries, to learn to live together. 'There is no such thing as pure justice in the real world,' suggests the late South African jurist and a former Minister of Justice, Dullah Omar. 'It is about fair play and the need to do what can be done to balance the books as best we can. This does not mean we ignore our obligation to deal with past crimes. It does mean we must not become so obsessed with the past that we neglect the future.'

Realistically, restorative justice is not an alternative to the established justice system. It seeks to recover certain neglected dimensions that make for a more complete understanding of justice. It asserts an inclusive and holistic notion of justice, refusing to reduce justice to retribution, while recognising the need to hold perpetrators accountable for crimes committed. At best, restorative justice is a process that encourages all those involved in a particular offence to resolve collectively how to deal with the aftermath of an offence and its implications for the future. It includes the restoration of the moral worth and human dignity of all people, which requires the emergence of a social order that provides for the basic needs of all citizens. This is a process to which victims, survivors and perpetrators, as well as those who benefited from past abuses, can contribute.

Recognising that restoration comes to different people in different ways, restorative justice is a difficult one. Some victims and their families demand criminal prosecutions while some claim the right to civil litigation. Some want the payment of monetary reparations. Many want to know why they were made to suffer and who killed their spouse, child or parent, wanting acknowledgement by the persons concerned. Others simply want to forget and get on with their lives.

Some perpetrators remain defiant and destabilising elements in society. Some simply withdraw from society. Others seek to share constructively in the new order, with some being ready to acknowledge their crimes and make such restitution where possible. Many who were not direct perpetrators, while benefiting from past abuses, want to forget while continuing to benefit. Others seek ways to share in the reconstruction of society.

The need to hold these positions in creative tension necessitates a level of statecraft that incorporates political compromise, acts of restorative and healing justice, retribution where appropriate and, not least, a level of inspired moral leadership. Restorative justice is self-consciously communal. It broadens the lens in the realm of justice, from 'me and my future' to 'we and our future'.

RETRIBUTIVE AND RESTORATIVE JUSTICE

Retributive justice is essentially concerned with crime as a violation of the law. It administers justice primarily as a corrective due to the state as the custodian of the rights of its citizens. Restorative justice views crime essentially as a violation of people and relationships between people. Its primary objective is to correct such violations and to restore relationships. As such, it necessarily involves victims and survivors, perpetrators and the community in the quest for a level of justice that promotes repair, trust-building and reconciliation. While the former seeks to apply the established law as a basis for reaffirming the legal basis for human decency, the latter draws attention to the need to create a milieu within which all those implicated in crime come to realise the need to uphold the principles of the law, co-operating in an endeavour to discern the best way to achieve this. It is essential that a transitional society establish the integrity of the state and the rule of law in the wake of an extended period of illegitimate rule and lawlessness. It is equally necessary to find a way in which victims, offenders and the broader community can co-operate in the correction of past wrongs. Both are required, the one depending on the other.

To this end, restorative justice involves three interrelated steps:

1. Inevitably, victimisation brings a desire for some kind of retribution. These emotions need to be addressed. The need to give expression to anger and resentment is appropriate and often therapeutic. Restoration is about seeking constructive ways of dealing with such emotions, recognising that unmitigated resentment and hatred can entrench a sense of victimhood and defeat. Retribution, at its best, however, involves more than a malicious desire for revenge. It requires the perpetrator to uphold the basic rules of human decency involved in any social contract for co-existence. Restorative justice explores ways of addressing this essential need by involving victims, perpetrators and the broader community in acts of restoration and rehabilitation.

2. Empathy and understanding, moral outrage and remorse, even

punishment, are at the same time not sufficient to restore the basis of a sustainable co-existence. Commensurate action, aimed at redressing the resentment and legitimate claims of victims and survivors, is required. This often includes some form of material compensation and programme of economic restoration.

3. Economic restoration by definition, requires trust and relationship-building. The likelihood of economic restoration is reduced in the absence of a minimum restoration of relationships between former enemies and antagonists. Personal and communal relations take time to restore. They are dependent on trust-building, barriers of separation being removed and people getting to know one another. Politically, this necessitates the forging of political structures. Economically, this often requires fair trade, labour protection, skills training and corrective employment practices.

RESTORATION AND TRANSITION

Restorative justice involves a holistic sense of justice. It demands more than is explicitly present in the immediate objectives of retributive justice. It offers a critique of retributive justice, which it sees as frequently failing to meet the broader rights of the victim, facilitate the reintegration of the perpetrator, or cultivate the essential values of a society. Recidivism rates, increases in crime and the perpetuation of violent social tendencies are identified as evidence of this.

The question is whether programmes of restorative justice are able to deliver inclusive justice more efficiently than established retributive forms of justice. Considered within the context of political transition, the pertinent question is whether initiatives such as truth and/or reconciliation commissions have succeeded in this regard. Have such initiatives created a national will and sufficient incentives to address the underlying causes of conflict that, for example, brought South Africa to the brink of collapse and have plunged some other countries into social and political chaos?

In many instances, such initiatives have contributed to the termination of overt forms of political violence, creating a space where peace-building and social transformation can take place. Evidence suggests that not all participants in the conflict have contributed to these processes as hoped. Staying with the South African transition, widely recognised as a prime example of restorative justice, the question needs to be asked whether this country's focus on reconciliation as a basis for restoration has in fact worked: not only politically but also at socio-economic levels. The question is whether the failure to place sufficient emphasis on socio-economic redress and structural correction has undermined the long-term prospects for social transformation. Herein lies the challenge facing restorative justice.

Restorative justice engages the question of how to generate sufficient incentive to ensure the holistic understanding of justice towards which it aspires. Archbishop Desmond Tutu, reflecting on the South African transitional process observed: 'Unless we are driven from within, by desire and persuasion, the chances are we will not rise to the material challenge that we face. The big stick, although appropriate in many situations, is insufficient. People need to be inwardly persuaded to do what we all know is ultimately in their self-interest.' Sometimes the threat of the big stick engenders the desire and persuasion to which the Archbishop refers. Restorative justice is ultimately about getting this balance right. It takes the wisdom of Solomon, the patience of Job and time. Such ingredients are rarely in abundance when victims have already waited too long and sacrificed too much in anticipation of a meaningful change.

Restorative justice rarely applies in a strictly semantic sense. To restore a situation to what it was before the onslaught of violence, let alone to some ideal sense of equality, is an impossible task. No amount of reparation or compensation can ever restore, to an individual or a community, what prevailed before a child was killed, a spouse murdered, a loved one raped or the worldly possessions of a family destroyed. The aim of restorative justice is rather to contribute to the rebuilding of society in a different way. It seeks to address the personal and communal dimensions that create the possibility of rebuilding life in the wake of tragedy and destruction. These include the re-empowerment and restoration of the dignity of victims and survivors, the restoration of civic trust and the affirmation of the right to such basics as food, housing, health-care and education.

Restorative justice is about democracy, good governance, peace, security, stability and justice, recognising that these are the essential building-blocks for the creation of socio-economic development. Conflict and development cannot be dealt with separately and need to be addressed through a comprehensive framework of governance that addresses root causes of conflict, as well as enabling those who have suffered most in conflict to participate in their own restoration. As such, it involves the creation of an environment that promotes sustainable development. When restorative justice succeeds in doing so, it offers the possibility of subjective and material reconstruction that retribution and related forms of justice can never accomplish on their own. It is this contribution that makes restorative justice an essential part of any transitional justice process.

Pieces of the Puzzle

FURTHER READING:

John Braithwaite, *Restorative Justice: Assessing an Immodest Theory and a Pessimistic Theory.* (Australian Institute of Criminology, Australia National University, 1998).

Jennifer Llewellyn and Robert Howse, *Restorative Justice: A Conceptual Framework.* (Ottawa: Law Commission of Canada, 1998).

Tony Marshall, *Restorative Justice: An Overview.* (London: Home Office Research Development and Statistics Directorate, 1999).

Larry Tifft and Dennis Sullivan, eds, *International Hand Book for Restorative Justice.* (New York: Routledge, 2005).

Howard Zehr, *Changing Lenses.* (Scotsdale, Pa: Herald, 1995).

6 Amnesty

Erik Doxtader

For countries divided by civil war, wracked by atrocity and faced with the daunting task of moving from a criminal regime to democracy, the contradictions of amnesty are not easy to resolve. In many situations, amnesty is simultaneously inevitable, valuable and unacceptable. If for no other reason than a lack of resources, post-conflict governments rarely have the capacity to prosecute every perpetrator of a gross human rights violation.

Amnesty can serve legitimate and important political ends. This is particularly true when it is used to assure members and influential supporters of an outgoing government that their release of power will not lead inexorably to their prosecution, imprisonment and perhaps execution. And yet, there is something fundamentally (morally) unsatisfactory about providing amnesty to those guilty of ordering and carrying out crimes against individuals, communities and humanity.

What of justice in the midst of transition? Do the functional benefits of amnesty justify abrogating the letter and spirit of domestic and international law? Are there conditions under which amnesty does not cultivate an ethic of impunity that confounds transition, provokes revenge and entrenches socio-political division? Can amnesty laws be designed to promote remembrance and an understanding of the past instead of the forgetting and denial that they so frequently appear to condone?

WHAT DOES AMNESTY DO?

Amnesty has long played a role in the history of human conflict. Today, amnesty is widely understood as a legislative or executive act that prohibits or prevents the prosecution of an individual or group for one or more (named or unnamed) crimes. Different from a pardon – a release from the punishment that follows a formal determination of guilt – amnesty is a common event. The most serious and controversial amnesties are those that appear in the wake of civil wars and during transitions from one form of government to another. Sometimes secret and other times public, amnesties in these situations may prevent criminal prosecutions and/or restrict the ability of victims to pursue civil damages for the harms that they have suffered. In an important essay (cited below), Ronald Slye has argued that these kinds of amnesties can take several forms:

1. *Amnesic or 'blanket' amnesties* provide individuals or groups with a broad protection from prosecution, often by a government that seeks to obscure the record of its atrocities. They provide little if any opportunity for the investigation of past abuses or the provision of redress to victims. Typically, the beneficiaries of such amnesties are not named publicly.

2. *Compromise amnesties* are more narrowly tailored than their amnesic counterparts. Frequently, they develop out of negotiations dedicated to creating a new government or building peace. Granted to particular groups of people or for specific kinds of action, compromise amnesties can shed some light on past crimes, particularly if they are carried out or attended by the work of a truth commission or other quasi-judicial body.

3. *Accountable amnesties* are those that involve the dedicated investigation and public disclosure of a crime. Offering both acknowledgement and compensation to victims, this kind of amnesty usually applies only to individuals and operates in accordance with a strict set of procedures and eligibility requirements. As the name suggests, it strives for accountability, the promotion of reconciliation and political transition that supports the protection of human rights.

WHEN IS AMNESTY JUSTIFIED? CAN IT EVER BE JUST?

When provided to those who have committed gross violations of human rights over the course of conflict, amnesty is a source of political, legal and moral controversy. In recent decades, this dispute has deepened as a result of amnesties granted by several Latin and South American governments and the advent of the International Criminal Court (ICC). Today, there is little consensus about the conditions under which perpetrators of gross human rights violations can justifiably be granted amnesty for their crimes. For human rights purists, the answer is rarely, if ever. In almost all cases, they contend, governments and the international community have a duty to prosecute: a duty that cannot be abrogated by practical considerations of transitional stability, resource constraints or non-retributive forms of justice. Beneath this strong objection to amnesty sits several specific arguments:

- Amnesty cultivates an ethic of impunity and forsakes accountability for criminal behaviour. This release from responsibility weakens the rule of law in post-conflict or transitional societies, creates incentives for informal retribution or revenge and undermines the very socio-political stability that amnesty claims to promote.
- Broad-based amnesties confound attempts to promote and cultivate respect for human rights. In many situations, it may undermine constitutional and international legal norms that are designed to help societies move from a deeply divided past to a democratic future.
- Many amnesty laws serve power at the expense of truth, hampering attempts to account for the scope, nature and causes of past human rights violations. This foreclosure of historical inquiry into why individuals or groups were targeted and what happened to loved-ones who were killed or abducted over the course of a conflict decreases the likelihood that adequate reparation will be paid to victims.
- Victims of gross human rights violations are victimised again as amnesties both violate their constitutional rights to seek redress from the courts, and limit opportunities for acknowledgement and meaningful reconciliation.

A strong presumption against the use of amnesty laws has not deterred their use. In part, this failure owes something to the relative weakness of international law, a shortcoming that may be remedied somewhat with the work of the ICC, and the growing support for the kinds of international war crimes tribunals that have been used in Rwanda, Sierra Leone and the former Yugoslavia. At a larger level, many contend that amnesty can play a constructive role in the delicate work of post-conflict transition, specifically as formal trials do not always fulfil their declared promise. In particular:

- The promise of amnesty can motivate authoritarian governments to negotiate their release of power, or appease opponents of political change who may otherwise seek to disrupt elections or other transitional mechanisms.
- In the midst of transition, amnesty may be useful in promoting social (re)integration and facilitating reconciliation. It may also conform with standing socio-cultural norms regarding the treatment of perpetrators.
- As adversarial justice is not always the best means to discover the truth of past human rights violations, amnesty may encourage the disclosure of past crimes and their motivation.
- Trials are costly and their outcomes are uncertain. In South Africa, for instance, several notorious members of the apartheid defence force were tried and acquitted at great expense to the state.
- In part due to narrow rules of evidence and a premium on formal procedure, trials tend to marginalise victims and foreclose opportunities for participation, acknowledgment and the recuperation of dignity.
- Some forms of amnesty may be well suited to the provision of restorative justice, especially if they recognise the needs of victims and ensure the payment of reparation.

THE SOUTH AFRICAN AMNESTY: PRECEDENT OR PROBLEM?

For those willing to consider the possibility that amnesty may be appropriate in some circumstances, there is an increasing consensus that it must be conditional, public and tied to formal measures of accountability and reparation. In this regard, the South African amnesty process has been held up as a potentially useful although far from perfect model.

Amnesty's role in the South African transition was discussed, debated and frequently ignored during the fragile negotiations that ended statutory apartheid. Only in December 1993, at the last possible moment and spurred partly by pressures from state security forces and the extreme right-wing, did the African National Congress (ANC) and government negotiators resolve the amnesty question. This agreement was then codified in the post-amble of the interim constitution:

> In order to advance such reconciliation and reconstruction, amnesty shall be granted in respect of acts, omissions and offences associated with political objectives and committed in the course of the conflicts of the past. To this end, Parliament under this Constitution shall adopt a law determining a firm cut-off date, which shall be a date after 8 October 1990 and before 6 December 1993, and providing for the mechanisms, criteria and procedures, including tribunals, if any, through which such amnesty shall be dealt with at any time after the law has been passed.

The meaning of this mandate was debated extensively during Parliament's creation of the Truth and Reconciliation Commission's (TRC) legislation and the Commission's early work. At base, the TRC's amnesty committee was charged to accept, hear and adjudicate amnesty applications from those who perpetrated gross human rights violations between May 1960 and May 1994. Detailed both in the Commission's governing legislation – The Promotion of National Unity and Reconciliation Act – and the TRC's *Final Report*, the criteria for granting amnesty revolved around the ability of applicants to:

- demonstrate that their acts or omissions constituted a gross human rights violation and were motivated by or intended to serve a political objective;
- make a full disclosure or a 'full and truthful account of the incidents in respect of which they were seeking amnesty'; and
- provide evidence that the means used to accomplish the act was proportional to the ends sought.

Slowed by a number of legal challenges from both perpetrators and victims and an unrealistic schedule for completing the hearings, the TRC's amnesty process extended well beyond the close of the larger Commission. Concluding only in 2002, its results were mixed. While it was envisaged that the threat of later prosecutions would motivate high-ranking apartheid officials to come forward, many declined to apply for amnesty, claiming variously that they were innocent, willing to take their chances or wary of the Commission's attitude and power.

The Amnesty Committee's *Final Report* indicates that it battled with the perception that it was 'perpetrator friendly' and that the procedures for hearing and adjudicating applications needed to be clarified earlier rather than later on in the process. After 1 888 days of hearings and granting 1 167 amnesties out of a total of 7 116 applications, the Committee argued that its work did provide a 'meaningful contribution to a better understanding of the causes, nature and extent of the conflicts and divisions of the past'.

While its ultimate relation to the edicts of international law remain uncertain, the rigours of the South African process did appear to overcome a number of challenges, including: the need for public hearings; opportunities for victim participation; and formal criteria designed to ensure perpetrator accountability for particular crimes. By the same token, the TRC was unable to motivate applications from the apartheid leadership and its ability to facilitate reconciliation may well have been hampered by the way in which its hearing took on a legal quality over time. Some of these difficulties may have had something to do with the Amnesty Committee's distance from the rest of the TRC, a separation that was partly mandated by the Commission's governing legislation.

In any event, the book remains open in several ways. For one, it appears that the present South African government will seek the selective indictment of some individuals who either refused to apply or were refused amnesty. Questions of how well the process worked, how much of the past it uncovered and how well it contributed to the provision of restorative justice remain important objects of study to this day.

AMNESTY'S DIFFICULT EQUATION

Amnesty is a controversial and perhaps inevitable element of transitional justice. In post-conflict situations, the need for amnesty is an indication of past criminality that cannot be overlooked and evidence that democratisation frequently occurs in moments when the rule of law is fragile, if not still in the making. Against this backdrop, however, there is little doubt that amnesty can have a better or worse form.

In the wake of the South African experience, a continuing task is to create domestic and international deterrents for those amnesties that hide the past and foster impunity, while creating incentives for transitional societies to grant amnesties only under strict criteria that are applied in public settings, geared toward revealing the truth of history, dedicated to ensuring accountability, and tied to the promotion of reconciliation and the timely provision of reparation. While an important step forward, it is important to remember that such efforts will not resolve amnesty's deeper dilemmas. Both an unjust forgiveness and the problem of how transitional societies wish to resolve the question of what can and cannot be forgiven, amnesty's equation does not easily sum. In this respect, amnesty's morality and legitimacy may hinge on whether it provokes sustained dialogue and debate over the ways in which the past can and should serve the future, and if it is accompanied by a dedicated effort to hear, acknowledge and honour the experiences of those who have suffered and no longer have the option of seeking redress from the law.

FURTHER READING:

Charles Villa-Vicencio and Erik Doxtader, eds, *The Provocations of Amnesty: Memory, Justice and Impunity.* (Cape Town: David Philip, 2003).

Diana Orentlicher, 'Settling Accounts: The Duty to Prosecute Human Rights Violations of a Prior Regime'. *Yale Law Journal*, 100 (1991).

Ronald Slye, 'The Legitimacy of Amnesties under International law and General Principles of Anglo-American Law'. V*irginia Journal of International Law*, 43 (2002), 174–247.

South African Truth and Reconciliation Commission. *Final Report*, Volume 6. (Cape Town, 2003).

7   Memory

Antjie Krog

46

German memory was like a big tongue
which kept on touching a painful tooth.

Normal history means: a plurality of interpretations.

Ian Buruma, *Wages of Guilt*

How does one reconstruct a society after conflict? How does one cut a community loose from the destruction of the past? Is it possible to rebuild a post-war society when those who should weave the social and moral fabric are themselves maimed? Add to this a fact shown by research that men, brutalised in conflict, bring violence and abuse into the domestic sphere. How then is maleness to be reconstructed? How does one prevent destroyed identities from affecting the third and fourth generation?

MY MEMORY

1.1   The year 1976 found me devastated. Left with divorce papers, a one-year-old child, scathing reviews of my latest poetry volume, I had not an iota of self-esteem left. In short, 1976 was my *annus horibilis*. I remember vaguely to have read somewhere, perhaps while washing clothes at a laundrette because I didn't buy newspapers at the time, that rioters were arrested in my hometown. Riots in that small town, I wondered briefly, before my personal failure, grief and misery overwhelmed me.

My memory of 1976 consisted of desperate attempts to climb out of the pits of depression, powerlessness and despair.

What I didn't know then was that I had only half a memory. A decontextualised memory.

1.2 Recently, I was contacted by Hélène Pastoors. She is a Belgian activist who spent 18 months in the infamous women prison in Kroonstad for assisting anti-apartheid activists. She was in prison and appeared in court while I was actually living in Kroonstad. She told me how she was taken to the magistrate's court and how a small group of comrades waved at her and shouted her name and how, in many ways, it kept her mentally sane. I was overcome by guilt. Why wasn't I among them? Those waving from behind police barricades? I was in that town during that time. It must have been in the newspapers. Why didn't I know?

Is it that I didn't want to know? It takes an extraordinary person to rise up against injustice. The ordinary person is afraid. The ordinary person cares for his or her own safety. So the memory does not remember that Hélène Pastoors was in the newspapers, does not remember a decision not to make any inquiries.

This is what one could call a refused-to-be-accommodated memory.

1.3 On a visit to Kroonstad I learnt that one of the women with whom I worked with shoulder-to-shoulder on school activities actually made the torture bags or sacks on her sewing machine which security police used to interrogate activists.

This is what one could call a it-didn't-but-it-should-have-formed-part-of-my-memory memory.

1.4 Since the democratic changes and Truth and Reconciliation Commission, my memory had been mostly restored. Books and programmes were presented on the student protests of 1976 – my own sad memories of that year are now bedded within a larger South African memory of the anger, devastation and turning point of the Soweto uprisings. I invited Hélène

Pastoors for dinner with several other Kroonstadters and we had a wonderful evening of laughter and stories. Her haunting image of Kroonstad and my guilt were touched in a positive way. Because people openly talk now of things that happened in the past, I got to know about the interrogation bag maker. I see her for what she is because she is no longer covered by the innocent white veneer of apartheid.

MY MOTHER'S MEMORY

2.1 These are some of my own personal memories. My mother, however, had her own set of memories, proving that one's brain and psyche is not an empty slate. What happens to you shapes not only your personality, but also your very brain functions.

My mother found herself one night being strangled in her bed. She started shouting, fighting and hitting while the grip tightened around her throat. Then per chance her hand touched the prickly shorn scalp and she realised it was her bloody great grandmother!

Everybody thought the great grandmother to be just an ordinary woman. The fact that she had shaved her head ever since the Anglo-Boer War and always wore a kind of skull-cap, was regarded as a sign of healthy mourning. The fact that two of her baby girls, born after the war, died, seemed part of her somewhat tragic life. After the attack that night on one of her great grandchildren, she was sent to an institution.

Years afterwards, the family found remnants of a diary that contained the following entry: 'The storm was raging through the night. The mortuary tent blown away. This morning they lay there. Row upon row of drenched corpses. Hair wild and eyes and mouths distended under the scorching sun. Among it, we saw the red plait of Aletta.'

Aletta was great grandmother's first-born. Then the family remembered that at least one of the babies who died had red hair like grandmother herself, and like my mother.

2.2 How does one reconstruct a society after conflict? How does one cut a community loose from the destruction of the past? Is it possible to rebuild a post-war society when those who should weave the social and moral fabric are themselves maimed? Add to this a fact shown by research that men, brutalised in conflict, bring violence and abuse into the domestic sphere. How then is maleness to be reconstructed? How can one prevent destroyed identities from affecting the third and fourth generation?

MY COUNTRY'S MEMORY

3.1 There are many different ways in which people accommodate the horror of their lives in their memories. Some simply don't know. To be able to live with what they're seeing, they don't see, so they have nothing to remember. The event was shut out before it could become a memory. The shutting out of the shutting out became the memory.

During the hearing of torturer Jeffrey Benzien, one of his victims, Gary Kruser, who was promoted to director in the new police force and placed in command of the VIP protection unit, asked permission to interrogate him.

Kruser: What happened after you arrested me?
Benzien: I didn't arrest you sir, perhaps you confuse me.
Kruser: I KNOW YOU. It was you!
Benzien: I do not remember ever arresting you.

After Benzien repeatedly denied having arrested Kruser, the latter broke down. It was clearly too much for flesh and feelings, that this experience which had nearly destroyed his life did not make the slightest imprint on Benzien's memory.

On the other hand, many of the victims who testified in the Western Cape mentioned Rambo – the feared security branch member who wore a red bandanna around his head when he lead casspirs into the townships driving in front in a red car. Although his lawyers tried to point out that he could not have been at certain events since he was on leave or still deployed elsewhere, the whole of the Western Cape had seen and experienced him. Does this mean that their memories were untrustworthy? Or had he merely become a symbol of all perpetrators; in other words: being present everywhere where brutality reigned.

At times people need the memory of others to affirm their own. Some Western Cape activists betrayed their comrades under torture. During the last throes of apartheid, different names had been circulated as being the traitors. One of these names was that of Gary Kruser. So, he wanted to know from Benzien:

Kruser: Did you ever get information out of me?
Benzien: No sir!
Kruser: Was anybody ever arrested because of me?
Benzien: No sir!

The relief on Kruser's face was plain to see. His own memory affirmed.

3.2 Some screen their memories and let those memories through that are true but somehow less traumatising – substituting those that cannot be brought to mind with those they can bear. Captain Jacques Hechter killed three people – one died while singing Nkosi Sikelel' iAfrika.

> **Judge Bernard Ngoepe**: Are you able to remember that on a certain day in 1987 on a farm near Pienaarsrivier, you electrocuted three people?
> **Hechter**: I can ... the electrocution ... I can remember after it was told to me. But it was completely out of my thoughts ... I consciously banned these things from my thoughts ... I haven't thought about it for ten years ...
> **Ngoepe**: But you remember trivialities.
> **Hechter**: Yes, I remember terribly ... I can remember the path ... it was a white chalky road ... and there were guinea-fowl. I can remember things like that, but really ... the worse deeds ... those I do not remember.

3.3 Others relive an incident in terms of flashbacks wherein an entire experience is re-enacted. The incident is kept separate from the conscious self in such a way as to preserve the latter intact and without it being integrated into the memory. And there is no warning sign that the flashback will occur, it simply happens.

Jeffrey Benzien's psychologist told me that Benzien was sitting outside on his veranda one evening, smoking a cigarette, when he had a flashback so intense and real that he burst into tears. This form of reliving formally repressed parts of one's memory often involves the experience of vivid imagery, usually visual in nature. Benzien's wife then called the psychologist who was working with him. But Benzien kept on saying to her: 'I cannot tell you – I'm too ashamed.' She said Benzien suffered from a severe form of self-loathing.

3.4 Another way of remembering is the retention of parts of an experience in such a fragmented way that it loses its meaning and no longer makes sense. These fragments can often block one's way in pursuing a relatively normal life, because undigested fragments of perceptions keep on breaking into the consciousness with no conscious meaning or relation to oneself.

Mrs Konile's son was one of the Guguletu 7. He was so blown apart by a hand grenade that she could only identify his feet. She testified:

Mrs Konile: After the funeral I was so miserable. I had nowhere to go. I live in a shack, it was very difficult. Something told me to go and pick up coals, it was on a Thursday. I was knocked down by a rock, this big rock hit me on my waist. I tried to move so that I could get some air ... When I woke up, I felt like I was just getting out of bed. And there was a continuous cry I could hear. It felt like I was going down–down–down. When I looked I was wet – wet – I was wet all over the place ... I said: 'Please urinate on a plate so that I can drink.' She did and then I regained consciousness.

3.5 Others allow their memories to 'colour' their current lives. If they have lost children or family through violent means they keep on fearing that it will happen again, in other words the traumatic legacy is lived out as one's inevitable fate.

3.6 Some people live with narratives that overpower their whole lives. It can obliterate any joy they might experience in their personal successes. The memory is frozen and cannot be interacted with. They have no sense of full living and are absorbed in the nightmare that forms the centre of their memory.

Deborah Matshoba: When I look around I marvel at how we battle to be normal ... and no one knows how shattered we are inside.

3.7 During the St James Massacre hearings, a white man testified as to how he was sitting in church and heard the door open and some strange noises. Then he saw his wife slumping across his lap and on her back he saw a red butterfly spreading slowly

across her yellow blouse. Butterfly! Was that not perhaps a bit too frivolous or care-free an image to describe how one's wife just got killed?

It took the man three years to arrive at that image, the psychologist told me afterwards. And the moment he got there, he could start the process of healing. To finally find words for a memory means to at last have handles on it. Then one can start manipulating it: put it aside when you no longer want to think about it instead of having it breaking into your life and thoughts, destroying efforts to lead a normal life.

MEMORY LOSS

4.1 The testimony of Jeffrey Benzien, the main torturer of the apartheid apparatus during the 1980s, gets the Truth and Reconciliation Commission to explore the notion of memory loss. Several perpetrators claim not to remember certain things and the Commission is obviously not sure whether these people are genuinely traumatised or whether they are deliberately hiding information and so do not fulfil their amnesty requirements of full disclosure.

4.2 To reconstruct one's memory, to beautify it, is an ordinary human trait, said the psychologists. Most people do it. One kind of memory loss is voluntary – one changes one's memory because one is under threat, because one cannot bear to live with the reality. Another kind is involuntary – something is so traumatic that it rips a hole in one's memory, and one really cannot remember the incident or what happened just before and after it.

AFFECTED MEMORY

5.1 It hurts to be part of the dominated, persecuted or despised group. That hurt is a constant pain, an intra-psychic pain, a constant awareness of the self as not being 'like them', being different and not being good enough.

That kind of pain apparently never leaves you and pervades your getting up, how you wait in a queue, your whole bearing during the day, how you go to bed and what you dream. You deeply desire to get rid of everything causing you this pain of being regarded as different.

5.2 So you try to defend yourself against this pain. But the dominant group is seldom vulnerable, can seldom be attacked as the source of distress, because it is often well ensconced in institutionalised privilege. Then the dominated turn inward against themselves and their communities. Men, humiliated in their jobs, internalise their impotence and then turn against their wives and children. Often wives allow the abuse because they are acutely aware of the rage of hopelessness burning away in their men. Hence the high levels of all forms of abuse evident in many oppressed and marginalised communities.

5.3 Damaged memories often lead to a psychological double-bind. For the sake of reconciliation, it is expected of you to be 'agreeable' – agreeable to nation-building, in the workplace or in your own neighbourhood. The dominated is now in a double-bind. He must be agreeable, but the moment he is agreeable, he knows that they think he is subservient, docile and acquiescent in his own oppression. If he is not 'agreeable', he will be labelled problematic, angry, aggressive, dangerous – feeding into the stereotypical representations of his community.

5.4 One of the outcomes of the double-bind experience is what is called the 'killing rage'. The repressed anger of having only one choice between sell-out and being kicked out, builds up in an individual to the extent that he lashes out in spurts of uncontrolled violence towards either other victims or members of the dominant group. But it can turn inward and manifest in forms of addiction and other destructive behavioural patterns.

5.5 The past can eat away at you. It can be a fire that consumes your soul.

CONVERSATION ABOUT MEMORY

6.1 'Why don't you forget, like this whole country is forgetting, and start afresh?' His black face is immobile.

'And find myself also surprised over the high crime, the violence in families, the moral chaos in South Africa and actually the whole of Africa? If you don't know where things come from, you won't be able to deal with them.'

'You misunderstood me. The only valid reason to keep remembering is to get a kind of moral immunity for yourself. And it goes like this: because this is the suffering recorded in my memory, I may do as I please. Because I suffered, I may now make others suffer and you dare not do anything to me.'

She is surprised at the direction the discussion is taking.

'My father was arrested during the apartheid years. To this day I hate to see him. He still has that look, of surrender and humiliation, and I cannot stand that. I refuse to live my life within this state of victimhood. I have bought him a separate house. Out of my way. But what I hate most is when I lash out against whites, he would say: all whites are not like that, and wants to tell me about a kind warder or other who gave him a newspaper. A newspaper for God's sake!'

'But maybe he knew whites in a more intimate way than you. He could distinguish between good and bad whites. You work here in a coloured business. How many whites do you know?'

'That is not the point. He is too soft on the likes of you. We, the children of that generation, we are more realistic. We are not interested in maybe there is a wonderful white person out there somewhere. We don't care. We want a country without whites.'

'Because you want to forget the past? And you know what: if you forget the past, before you wipe your eyes out, you will be as racist as the whites ever were. The solution lies not in forgetting or ignoring the past, because then you run the risk of becoming a racist yourself, providing you with a future no better than the past you've just struggled to overthrow. Like a drug addict with a destroyed memory. Because you cannot remember, you will not be able to imagine a new kind of life for yourself.'

CONCLUSION

7.1 **Albie Sachs**: 'We want our memories confirmed. Previously we were castigated for being wrong; now we want to be affirmed for being right.'

We need our memories to be in the prism of many lights, because it is dangerous to hoist one's memory as the only memory, and the memory for all people at all times.

We also need to learn how to read memories. To make a distinction between what felt right and wonderful (or horribly wrong) and the context in which it took place. I have the most blissful memories of innocence on a beach with my father – but the fact that the beach was for whites only brings another frame to that memory.

7.2 We also need to distinguish the role of myth in memory. How myth validates one's experience from a particular, often ethnic, point of view: black people don't care for their children, they call anybody my son or my mother and they have these extended families – so it is okay to have a woman work for you 24 hours a day, or bring a man to the mines without his family.

7.3 But above all we need our memories restored after a past of conflict. We need to be aware of all the other memories, of victims and perpetrators alike; we need to understand that every single one of them is hurt in a particular way. If we want a future of living together in peace towards prosperity, we need all memories to be healed as far as possible.

7.4 An individual's identity involves a complex interplay of multiple spheres such as the interpersonal, the ethnic, the occupational, the economical, political, national, etc. These parts of a person co-exist dynamically to create a continuous conception of life from past through present to future. Ideally, the individual should simultaneously have free psychological access to and movement within all these dimensions of identity. Exposure to trauma causes a rupture in the personality so that the person no longer has free and easy access to these dimensions.

7.5 Trauma is being carried over from generation to generation by words, memories, body language, silences and personal scars. God visits the iniquity of the fathers upon the children unto the third and fourth generation of those that displease and reject Him, but shows mercy unto generations of those that love Him and keep His commandments. God banished the Israelites to 40 years in the desert, because he did not want those who KNEW the past, knew slavery to build the Promised Land.

7.6 Morality usually acquires form through what the majority in a community deems to be the appropriate or the right way of conduct or behaviour. These codes gradually evolve as a community lives through and remembers its history. If there is no coherent and cohesive communal text of memory, then it becomes impossible for people to live together. If groups with different and competing memories are being forced to live together like in the Middle East, or are living apart like in South Africa, it becomes crucial to develop a historical narrative that not only accommodates the variety of memories, but in the process rectifies one-sided distortions which perpetuate the spiral of conflict.

FURTHER READING:

Yael Danieli, ed., *International Handbook of Multigenerational Legacies of Trauma*. (Kluwer, 1998).

Ian Buruma, *Het Loon van de Schuld*. (Amsterdam: Atlas, 1994).

Caroline Moser and Fiona C Clark, eds, *Victims, Perpetrators or Actors? Gender, Armed Conflict and Political Violence*. (London: Palgrave, 2001).

Tamar Fox, *Inherited Memories – Israeli Children of Holocaust Survivors*. (London: Cassell, 1999).

Shosana Felman and Dori Laub, *Testimony – Crises of Witnessing in Literature, Psychoanalysis, and History*. (New York: Routledge, 1992).

8   Testimony

Fiona Ross

58 To 'testify' means to bear witness, to give truthful evidence or to state
formally that something is true. Testifying is often accompanied by an
oath that signifies a commitment to truth and truthfulness. The oath
links the person to his or her word, holding person and word hostage
to a higher force. On the face of it, these do not seem complicated
notions. They imply that both testimony itself and the information it
conveys are significant and worthy of public attention and that the
testifier agrees to be accountable for the veracity of his or her telling.

As a form of truth-telling, testimony in its modern form rests
heavily on witnessing, particularly an eye-witnessing to the events
in question. In this model, truth is identified through a relation
of proximity to an event. In antiquity, however, testimony implied
martyrdom. In part, this was because testifying involves risk.
Philosopher Michel Foucault points out that in ancient Greece,
frank speech (truthfulness) was not an attribute of the information
conveyed but of the teller's character. In order to testify to the truth,
individuals had to have specific moral qualities, particularly bravery.
Truth-telling required courage because it frequently involved
speaking critically of institutions and established forms of power.
Moreover, truth-tellers had to be citizens (which meant that they
were free men; women and slaves could not be citizens) and they
needed a well-developed sense of duty and a sense of certainty
about the truth they told.

Nowadays, witnessing is a central element of judicial proceedings. In addition to their function in courts, testimonial practices have taken on a significant role in public life, especially in conditions of oppression or political instability. In such instances, testimonial practices have played an important role in garnering information about wrongs committed and not acknowledged by the state. Throughout Latin America in the 1980s and 1990s, for instance, testimonies were collected as part of a methodology of collating data about state abuses during periods of undemocratic rule. Testimony was, of course, a central component in the methodology of South Africa's Truth and Reconciliation Commission (TRC). Increasingly, those who appear before such commissions speak about their own personal experiences. They are not disinterested and impartial witnesses but were participants, affected deeply by that which they describe.

WHAT DOES TESTIMONY OFFER?

Broadly speaking, there are two contradictory models of bearing witness. First, there is an assumption that talk heals – that is, that there is a positive relation between speech and recuperation. Built into this are other assumptions, namely: that testimonies accurately represent experience; that all experiences can be represented in words and that everyone will comprehend them; that these anticipated effects of speech are both stable and durable; that once spoken, words will be accepted as neutral and as an accurate reflection of events; and that the healing effects which may accrue to the individual will also accrue to the society as a whole. These are the kinds of assumptions that underpin truth commissions. Such forums hold that testimony involves a universal ritual of healing which has the function of uniting individual experience with large-scale social processes. Testifying is thought to relieve individual suffering by giving voice to experience, a process that, it is hoped, will promote healing at an individual and a social level.

Simultaneously, testimony may facilitate the collection of data that can be used to hold those responsible for harm to account. The South African TRC used this model of testimony, especially in that it rested on the assumption that there is a healing relationship between words and experience. Equating testimony with truth and truth with healing at the levels of both individual and society, the Commission's report recognised that not all testimony heals but added that 'Many ... were able to reach towards healing by telling the painful stories of their pasts.'

Second, the literature on testimony demonstrates that at the heart of some kinds of extreme experience, such as torture or absolute horror, language itself fails to convey either experience or meaning. It is not always easy or even possible to speak of some forms of suffering; some experiences remain 'unsayable'. We learn too, that sometimes people choose not to tell of their experiences: worried about the effects on future generations, they hold them within. This is particularly the case where peoples' experiences run counter to the ideals that society holds. One example is of women who have been sexually violated and who realise that speaking out may expose them to humiliation and shame in societies where women are undervalued or are blamed for men's violent actions. Additionally, language does not always adequately allow for the description of experience; some experiences are simply too horrifying to relive in the telling although they may continue to haunt. There may be conflict between the urge to identify facts and the desire to tell 'to the fullest extent' of one's experiences. The model that underpins truth commissions does not take account of long-term effects of testifying in public. It does not anticipate competing versions of the same events or conflicting interpretations. It also does not anticipate that some kinds of experience, such as sexual violation or humiliations that undermine local models of manhood, may be difficult to translate into public speech.

As a form of truth-telling, testimony has also generated a great deal of suspicion among historians and social analysts. Testimony's forms and claims are contested. What is truth? What kind of evidence suffices to make truthful claims about events? Can subjective states, such as emotions, serve as evidence in courts of law or in history books? Many historians and social analysts distrust testimony's subjective and individual nature. They also distrust the source of testimony: memory, and its reference to the self. We know that memory is not the simple transference of experience into a transparent record but is complicated by the contexts of recall, desire and intention. Historians have long asked about the reliability of an individual's memory of events. They have also asked about the relation of individual memory to social processes. Does an individual's memory offer sufficient grounds for assertions about the nature of reality and experience?

Together, these questions have stimulated research across a variety of settings into the nature of testimonies, the forms of language in

which truth claims are made and the rules of genre through which their veracity is assessed. They alert us to be on the lookout for local forms of expression that may not mesh neatly with the more formal requirements of, for example, the courts, where testifiers' truth claims are not taken at face value but are open to scrutiny and contestation.

HOW CAN WE UNDERSTAND TESTIMONY IN THE SOUTH AFRICAN CONTEXT?

Learning of intimate experience was a central aim of the South African TRC's work of ascertaining the truth concerning gross violations of human rights. To this end, it employed a testimonial method, inviting approximately ten percent of respondents 'to tell their stories' in public hearings held by the Human Rights Violations Committee. Storytelling was often depicted as an authentically African methodology, a mode of communication that Archbishop Tutu describes as central to religion and to African traditions.

These traditions include diverse practices of conflict resolution in which events are narrated by protagonists, mediated to find creative solutions, and funerary practices enacted in which the life of the deceased person is narrated by kinsfolk or friends. Yet, the model of testimony as storytelling – 'telling to the fullest extent' – used in the TRC's work owes as much to large-scale processes of modernity – which includes proselytising Christianity, psychotherapy and modern judicial processes – as it does to local traditions. As a process that drew from and responded (not always effectively) to local contexts, the TRC's testimonial process drew on a potent mix of medical, legal and religious metaphors, and local conventions of speech.

At present, there are two main models of the testimonial form. The first suggests that testimony is the natural expression of intrinsic truths. Often tied to psychotherapeutic interventions, it anticipates that stories of pain already exist intact within the sufferer and that all that is required is a 'safe space' within which they can be released. A second model holds that testimonies are genres of speech, and that their effective performance rests on their adherence to the implicit rules associated with these genres. For example, some testifiers before the TRC spoke in ways that would be associated with courtroom proceedings: clear, to the point, direct and factual. Others drew on models more commonly associated with African traditions of story and speech: elliptical, full of pause and repetition, their cadence and rhythm markedly different to the clipped style favoured by the courts. Some people were able to wield words with great effect. Confident of the story they told, their words speak powerfully. Others were more hesitant in speaking of violence and suffering.

The difference between these modes draws attention to the complexity of listening to testimonies. In South Africa, testimonies offered before the TRC were both standardised in their form and idiosyncratic in their representations of individual experience. People testified for different reasons, and their pull to speech may have encouraged them to reveal things they might not otherwise have revealed, or to conceal that which remains painful to themselves, or which they fear might harm others. Drawn from testifiers through empathy, questioning and sometimes through almost unbearable probing, the testimonies offered before the TRC are best seen as co-creations: stories that weave together personal experience and diverse narrative conventions, subjecting them to the dictates of a single genre of speech. Heard by ears unaccustomed to the specifics of historical context and local narrative models, testimonies can be confusing. Indeed, much rests on the unspoken. Testifiers at the TRC frequently spoke of their everyday contexts in ways that resonated with local audiences, but which were confusing to those less familiar with the particularities of context or modes of speech.

The complexities that arise from the intersection of local forms of expression and standardised genres are not singular to South Africa. We should not be misled into thinking that testimony is neutral. It is carefully produced in specific contexts and at specific times. This does not mean that it has no truth-value or is not factual, but it does hint at the extent to which the conditions that produce speech and silence of varying kinds are important in shaping how experience is worded. Understanding testimony in this way, rather than in terms of a model that holds that testimony is intact and awaiting only the opportunity to emerge, is useful in that it leads us carefully to assess not only the content of testimonies, but the conditions of possibility that make testimonial interventions possible, likely and effective.

What testimony offers, then, is a record of subjective experience: the experience of the world and of events as they affect oneself and those close to one. This is important. The writing of history has long rested on a distinction between subjective and objective, with the historian's task being an objective account of events and processes. The inclusion of testimonies, as one way of recording history, restores to the historical record a sense of the ways that people experience the times and events they live through and make. Testimonies are usually offered with the hope of making a difference – to individual lives, to social relations and to the records held in an archive. Indeed, personal accounts such as those offered in testimonies are becoming important ways in which we teach children about the past. Such accounts offer multiple perspectives on past events.

CONCLUSION

Individual testimonies may facilitate greater understanding of experiences. By offering a way to understand the effects of large-scale processes – violence, apartheid and economic disempowerment – on the intimacies of everyday life, they are an important means through which individuals express experience. However, a collection of testimonies does not make for a clear and unambiguous assessment of the past. Testimonies cannot do this alone. It requires careful analysis to show the threads and connections that link experiences and, in the absence of such analysis, explanation and interpretation, testimonies remain divergent accounts of the past. This is not necessarily negative: keeping histories open to reinterpretation is important; divergent testimonial accounts enable this process. While their multiplicity is valuable, it can be confusing for those wishing to drawn definite conclusions or to make unambiguous moral judgements.

Yet, while lauding the ways that testimony enables inclusion of the everyday experiences of suffering and resistance into historical narratives, we need to be wary of too easy a conflation of individual speech and individual healing and between these processes and social repair. Testimonies whose contents approximate social ideals are likely to be validated, but when people speak of experiences that counter such ideals, they may find that the process of testifying actually undermines them. We need to remember that when testimonies go against the grain of convention, individuals may feel exposed and vulnerable. And too often, reparative measures are slow in coming, undermining the reasons for which people testify.

There is a danger that testimonial practices shaped by conventional understandings of history and experience will limit the range of expression, reassert conventional understandings or re-inscribe old dichotomies. The diversity of testimonial practices calls for careful attention not only to what is said but also to what is left out of formal speech, to who speaks and who is silent. That is, it calls for close attention to the ways that stories of experience are offered, held within, silenced or erased from the historical record. We need to understand both the forms of language that are used to convey experience and the intersections of the idiosyncratic with the conventional in individuals' speech and silence.

Pieces of the Puzzle

FURTHER READING:

Ingrid Agger, *The Blue Room: Trauma and Testimony among Refugee Women.* (London: Zed, 1994).

A Douglass and T Vogler, eds, *Witness and Memory: The Discourse of Trauma.* (New York and London: Routledge, 2003).

Fiona C Ross, *Bearing Witness: Women and the Truth and Reconciliation Commission in South Africa.* (London: Pluto, 2003).

Elaine Scarry, *The Body in Pain: The Making and Unmaking of the World.* (New York: Oxford University Press, 1985).

Richard Werbner, Smoke from the Barrel of a Gun: Postwars of the Dead, Memory and Re-inscription in Zimbabwe. *Memory and the Postcolony: African Anthropology and the Critique of Power*, R Werbner, ed. (London: Zed, 1998), 71–102.

TRANSITIONAL JUSTICE

SECTION 2

9   Transitional Justice

Alex Boraine

Transitional justice seeks to address challenges that confront
societies as they move from an authoritarian state to a form of
democracy. Frequently, these societies are emerging from serious
conflict and violence that often includes widespread human rights
violations and, in some instances, genocide and crimes against
humanity. Such situations are often characterised by a breakdown in
legal services; stark divisions and apportioning of blame; institutional
collapse; and economic downturn. In this light, transitional justice is
not a contradiction of criminal justice, but rather a deeper, richer
and broader vision of justice which seeks to confront perpetrators,
address the needs of victims, and start a process of reconciliation
and transformation toward a more just and humane society.

The Nuremberg Trials, the International Tribunal for Former
Yugoslavia and the International Tribunal for Rwanda, as well as the
establishment of the Permanent International Criminal Court (ICC),
are themselves major steps forward in the effort to confront impunity.
They are also a stern reminder to those prepared to commit serious
criminal acts that they will face grave sanctions if and when they are
brought to book.

However, realistically it is impossible to prosecute all offenders
during times of transition. Who then should be prosecuted? This
vexed question of selective prosecution is one that seems to
undermine the very idea of individual criminal responsibility so

fundamental to our understanding of the rule of law. Other problems also abound. In the wake of conflict, national legal systems are often in disarray and trials are often both very lengthy and costly. Moreover, the almost exclusive focus by tribunals on the perpetrator(s) is often to the detriment of the victim(s). In short, the aim of transitional justice is wider than prosecuting perpetrators. Punishment cannot be the last word.

Due to these shortcomings, it is impossible to deal with the true intent of justice by court procedures alone. A holistic approach to transitional justice seeks to complement retributive justice with restorative justice.

There are at least five components of this holistic approach:

1. Accountability

The rule of law and the fair administration of justice deserve our greatest respect. No society can claim to be free or democratic without strict adherence to the rule of law. Dictators and authoritarian regimes abandon the rule of law at the first opportunity and resort to brazen power politics leading to all manner of excess. It is of central importance, therefore, that those who violate the law are punished. But there are limits to the law and we need to embrace a multi-faceted notion of justice that is wider, deeper and richer than retributive justice.

It is not only impossible to prosecute all offenders, but an overzealous focus on punishment can make securing sustainable peace and stability more difficult. To achieve a just society, more than punishment is required. Documenting the truth about the past, restoring dignity to victims and embarking on the process of reconciliation are all vital elements of a just society. Equally important is the need to transform society so that it does not impede the consolidation of democracy and the creation of a human rights culture. It follows that approaches to societies in transition will be multi-faceted and will incorporate the need for consultation to realise the goal of a just society.

2. Truth Recovery

One of the non-judicial mechanisms that has gained great prominence over the last ten years is the Truth and Reconciliation Commission (TRC). A TRC, as indicated by its title, is concerned first and foremost with the recovery of truth. Through truth-telling, these commissions attempt to document and analyse the structures and methods used in carrying out illegal repression, while taking into account the political, economic and social contexts in which violations have occurred. In some ways, it is unfortunate that the word 'truth' is used. Beyond its Orwellian overtones, many critics rightly point out that it is impossible for the truth ever to be fully known.

3. Reconciliation

A number of commissions have talked not only about *truth* but also about *reconciliation*. If the word truth conjures up problems for many people, so does the word reconciliation. It has religious connotations, especially in the Christian faith, and there are many who would prefer that the word and the concept of reconciliation not be used in TRCs that are seeking to recover the truth and promote the interests of victims.

At best, reconciliation involves commitment and sacrifice; at its worst, it is an excuse for passivity, for siding with the powerful against the weak and dispossessed. Religion, in many instances, has given a bad name to reconciliation, representatives often having joined forces with those who exploited and impoverished entire populations, instead of being in solidarity with the oppressed.

Reconciliation is unrealistic when it calls for mere forgetting or concealing. In Argentina, the concept of reconciliation is regarded with deep scepticism. In that country, the Roman Catholic Church, in large measure, supported the military junta, and the perpetrators of human rights violations were always the first to call for reconciliation. The same is true of Rwanda, where religious groups and officials participated in the massacre of the Tutsis. In this context, talk about reconciliation is highly suspect and can be viewed as a call for amnesia. Unless calls for reconciliation are accompanied by acknowledgement of the past and the acceptance of responsibility, they will be dismissed as cheap rhetoric.

Perhaps one of the ways in which to achieve at least a measure of reconciliation in a deeply divided society is to create a common memory that can be acknowledged by those who created and implemented the unjust system, those who fought against it and the many more who, while in the middle, claimed not to know what was happening in their country.

Reconciliation, as a process for seeking an often elusive peace, must be understood through the lens of transitional justice. It is better understood if victims believe that their grievances are being heard and addressed, that the silence is being broken. Reconciliation can begin when perpetrators are held accountable, when truth is sought openly and fearlessly, when institutional reform commences and when the need for reparation is acknowledged and acted upon. The response by former victims to these initiatives can increase the potential for stability and increase the chances of a sustainable peace.

The process of reconciliation has often been hindered by the silence or denial of political leaders concerning their own responsibilities and the failures of the state. On the other hand, when leaders are prepared to speak honestly and generously about their own involvement or, at least, the involvement of their government or the previous government, then the door is open for the possibility of some reconciliation amongst the citizens.

4. Institutional Reform

For truth and reconciliation to flourish, serious and focused attention must be given to both individuals and institutions. Institutional reform should be at the very heart of transformation. The TRC is an ideal model for holding together both retrospective truth and prospective needs. Unfortunately, most TRCs have chosen to focus almost entirely on individual hearings. This is important and critical, but if commissions were to hold institutional hearings, it would enable them to call to account those institutions directly responsible for the breakdown of the state and the repression of citizens.

In at least one commission, an opportunity was created for spokespersons from the military, the police and the security forces while also inviting politicians, faith communities, legal representatives, the media and labour officials to give an account of their role in the past and how they saw their role in the future. In other words, it is simply not enough to be merely concerned about the past. We must deal with it, but we must not dwell in it. We should deal with the past for the sake of the future.

On a recent visit to Serbia, it was obvious that one of the major problems preventing the country from moving on from its dark and ominous past was that its institutions had remained almost exactly the same: the same policemen were controlling the police forces; the same generals were controlling the army. This can be said to be true of most of Serbia's major institutions. As I moved from one group of leaders to another, it became clear that unless these institutions are radically restructured, there will be little opportunity for growth, development or peace in Serbia. This is not only true of Serbia but applies to the former Yugoslavia as a whole and to all states in transition.

In deeply divided societies where mistrust and fear still reign, there must be bridge-building and a commitment to both criminal and economic justice. For that to be a reality, institutions as well as individuals have to change.

5. Reparations

Reparations have a long history, but until now have not received sufficient systematic attention. The individual reparations issued by the Federal Republic of Germany were a watershed moment in the history of reparations. Until 1952, reparations were solely an inter-state affair, involving payments by the losing state to the victorious one, as in the Versailles Treaty. Reparations to the victims of the Holocaust were the first instance of a massive nationally sponsored reparations programme to individuals who had suffered gross human rights violations.

It is worth emphasising that from the standpoint of the victims, reparations programmes occupy a special place in a transition to democracy. Reparations are, for them, the most tangible manifestation of the efforts of the state to remedy the harms they have suffered. Criminal justice, even if it were completely successful, both in terms of the number of perpetrators brought to book (far from being the case in any transition) and of the results (which are always affected by the availability of evidence and by the persistent weaknesses of judicial systems), is in the end a struggle against perpetrators rather than an effort on behalf of victims.

From truth-telling, victims can obtain significant benefits that may include a sense of closure derived from knowing the fate of loved ones, and a sense of satisfaction from the official acknowledgement of that fate. But in the absence of other positive and tangible manifestations, truth by itself can easily be considered an empty gesture – as cheap and inconsequential talk. Finally, institutional reforms will always be a long-term project, which only indirectly affect the lives of the victims.

In many ways, the dilemmas and challenges in reparations are a microcosm of the overall challenges of transitional justice. How does one balance competing legitimate interests in redressing the harms of victims and ensuring the democratic stability of the state? Similar to other areas of transitional justice, such as truth-telling or institutional reform, simple judicial decisions cannot provide the comprehensive solutions demanded by such interests. Rather, solutions must be found in the exercise of judgement and a creative combination of legal, political, social and economic approaches.

CONCLUSION

There are enormous difficulties in pursuing justice in a normal situation, but when one attempts to do this in countries undergoing transitions, the problems are intensified. There is a need to balance two imperatives: on the one hand, there is the need to return to the rule of law and the prosecution of offenders; on the other, there is a need for rebuilding societies and embarking on the process of reconciliation. In helping to make states work, it is important, therefore, to balance accountability with the shoring up of fragile emerging democracies. The overall aim should be to ensure a sustainable peace, which will encourage and make possible socio-economic development.

FURTHER READING:

Donald Shriver, *An Ethic for Enemies* (Oxford: Oxford University Press, 1995).

Ruti Teitel, *Transitional Justice.* (Oxford: Oxford University Press, 2000).

Robert Rotberg and Dennis Thompson, eds, *Truth versus Justice: The Morality of Truth Commissions.* (Princeton: Princeton University Press, 2000).

10 Genocide

Jeremy Sarkin

Genocide has been called the crime of crimes. It has occurred throughout history, although there are those who suggest that some events have incorrectly been labelled genocide because they do not see these events as complying with the present legal definition of genocide. This debate continues to play itself out in the 21st century, with some arguing that present events in, for example, the Democratic Republic of the Congo (DRC) and Sudan constitute genocide. Others contend that although these events are horrific, they do not comply with the international legal definition.

One reason for the disagreements about the extent to which genocide occurred in the past is that legal genocide convictions occurred for the first time only in the 1990s. Prior to the establishment of the International Criminal Tribunals for Rwanda and the former Yugoslavia, there were no courts to prosecute those guilty of committing genocide. Few countries had this crime on their statute books, although some prosecuted individuals were charged with murder and other types of domestic crime. Thus, while genocide was deemed to be the most terrible of crimes, the fact that there was no forum to prosecute those guilty of it resulted in some regarding genocide as a crime that existed in theory rather than practice. In brief, the lack of court decisions on genocide, resulted in a lack of clarity regarding its interpretation and practical application in specific settings.

EGLISE
SITE DU GENOC

NTARAM

GENOCIDE SITE

KIRIZIYA

AHABEREYE

N'ITSEMBATSEMB

NTARAMA

DE : ± 5000 PERSONNES

CHURCH

± 5000 PERSONS

NTARAMA

TSEMBABWOKO

RY'ABANTU BARENGA 5000

INTERNATIONAL DEBATE

Today, together with crimes against humanity and war crimes, genocide is an international crime. Often these crimes overlap. The major difference between genocide and crimes against humanity is that genocide requires a specific mental intention by the person or persons who carry out the deed. Specifically, genocide requires 'the specific intent to eliminate, in whole or in part, a particular group that is specifically designated in the law.' In addition, while there can be overlap, the prohibition of genocide serves to protect certain specified groups from extermination while crimes against humanity exist mainly to protect a civilian population from persecution. Crimes against humanity are seen as crimes with a much older vintage, and until the Genocide Convention was drafted in the 1940s, most saw genocide merely as a sub-category of crimes against humanity.

The word 'genocide' comes from the Greek word *genos (geno)*, which means race or tribe, and the Latin word *caedere (cide)* which means killing. Thus, in broad non-legal language, the word is meant to signify the killing of a tribe or race. When it was coined in the 1940s by Raphael Lemkin, the term provoked significant debate, not least because the notion of genocide was unknown before then. Given ensuing uncertainty over whether or not genocide was a crime before World War II, the Nuremberg laws that were used to prosecute those responsible for atrocities committed during wartime did not contain the crime of genocide. While they were handed down for war crimes and crimes against humanity, many of the convictions at Nuremberg were for crimes that would today be termed genocide. It is clear that the crime existed long before the word was used, with the Genocide Convention specifically stating that the crime existed before the Convention, and that it exists as a crime separate from the Convention.

THE GENOCIDE CONVENTION

The main provisions relating to the definition and prohibition of genocide are found in the Convention for the Prevention and Punishment of the Crime of Genocide of 1948. There are also provisions relating to genocide in the Statutes of the International Criminal Tribunals for Rwanda and the former Yugoslavia, as well as the Statute of the International Criminal Court (ICC).

Crucially, Article One of the Genocide Convention states that genocide is an international crime that can be committed in time of war or peace. The language and provisions of the Genocide Convention have been imported into the Statutes of the two Tribunals as well as the ICC. It is generally accepted, however, that the provisions outlawing genocide have assumed the status of customary international law. Article Four of the Convention provides that individuals guilty of committing genocide shall be punished, regardless of whether they are constitutionally responsible rulers, public officials or private individuals. A number of provisions impose obligations on states that are party to the Convention to enact domestic measures to prevent and punish genocide. The Convention also has mechanisms for states to call upon organs of the United Nations to take action to prevent and suppress genocide, and to refer disputes concerning the 'interpretation, application or fulfilling' of the Convention to the International Court of Justice.

Article Two of the Genocide Convention defines genocide as an act committed with the *intent* to destroy, in whole or in part, a national, ethnical, racial or religious group, such as:

- killing members of the group;
- causing serious bodily or mental harm to members of the group;
- deliberately inflicting on the group conditions of life calculated to bring about its physical destruction in whole or in part;
- imposing measures to prevent births within the group;
- forcibly transferring children of one group to another.

Each group that enjoys specific protection in terms of the Convention, and now elsewhere, has been specifically enumerated, but it has taken the various recent decisions of the two International Criminal Tribunals to determine the composition of these groups. Thus, the International Criminal Tribunal for Rwanda has noted that people who share a common language or culture can define an ethnic group. A religious group's members 'share the same religion, denomination or mode of worship' while members of a national group usually share a common citizenship. Members of a racial group can be distinguished by hereditary physical traits that are often linked to a geographical region, 'irrespective of linguistic, cultural, national or religious factors'. Thus, genocide is composed of three elements:

1. the commission of any of the acts in Article Two;
2. the direction of that act at one of the enumerated types of groups; and
3. the intent to destroy the group in whole, or in part.

INTERNATIONAL CRIMINAL COURT (ICC)

Recently, there have been several important developments that bear on the definition and prosecution of genocide. For instance, the crime of genocide is found in the Statute of the ICC. Thus, for the first time, it can be prosecuted when it occurs, regardless of where, although there are jurisdictional requirements with respect to where it took place and whether a country is a party to the Statute or not. In this regard, one of the most important countries that has not ratified the Treaty, and in fact is making an active effort to ensure that other countries do not become State parties to the Court, is the United States of America. One further issue of importance is that while genocide is one of the crimes that the ICC will be able to prosecute, the Statute does not have retrospective effect and thus the Court can only prosecute acts of genocide that occurred after the Statute came into force on 1 July 2002.

As a result of the two international tribunals and the fact that they have handed down a number of convictions, the jurisprudence about the meaning and characteristics of genocide has grown significantly. The development of this body of law has been assisted by the fact that a number of countries, in line with their obligations as members of the ICC, have enacted genocide as a crime in their own countries. Thus, the law has grown as cases have emerged in domestic settings. In Sierra Leone, Cambodia and East Timor, hybrid courts that operate as both international and domestic courts have also contributed to the growing jurisprudence on international crimes and the procedures for their enforcement.

CONCLUSION

The definition of genocide is now settled law and is contained in international customary law, the Genocide Convention, the Statute of the two international criminal tribunals and in the Statute of the ICC. It can now can be enforced and thus the fact that it can, and that it must because of state obligations to either prosecute or extradite those responsible, ensures for the first time that those who want to perpetrate this crime may be deterred from doing so. While the law on genocide is often seen to be only a matter for criminal law, victims are also using the law in an attempt to obtain reparation. For example, victims have sued perpetrators in a number of countries, including in countries with no connection to the actual genocide, such as the United States. Clearly then there is greater clarity on what constitutes genocide and greater likelihood that those who perpetrate it will be held accountable both criminally and civilly.

FURTHER READING:

Howard Ball, *Prosecuting War Crimes and Genocide: The Twentieth-century Experience.* (Lawrence: University Press of Kansas, 1999).

Israel W Charny, 'Toward a Generic Definition of Genocide'. In *Genocide: Conceptual and Historical Dimensions*, George J Andreopoulos, ed., (Philadelphia: University of Pennsylvania Press, 1994).

Jeremy Sarkin, 'Finding a Solution for the Problems Created by the Politics of Identity in the Democratic Republic of the Congo (DRC): Designing A Constitutional Framework for Peaceful Co-Operation'. In: *The Politics of Identity.* (Konrad Adenhauer Foundation, 2001).

11 The International Criminal Court

Ronald Slye

The International Criminal Court (ICC) was created by a treaty
negotiated in Rome in 1998 (the Rome Treaty). The Rome Treaty
required 60 ratifications before the Court could come into
existence. These ratifications came far sooner than many had
anticipated and on 1 July 2002, the ICC came into being. As of
May 2004, 94 countries had ratified the Rome Treaty. These include
38 states from Europe, including France, Germany and the United
Kingdom; 24 states from Africa, including the Democratic Republic
of the Congo, Namibia, Nigeria, South Africa and Sierra Leone; and
other significant states from all regions of the globe, including
Argentina, Australia, Brazil, Canada, Jordan and New Zealand.
Significant states that have *not* ratified the treaty include China,
Russia and the United States.

The Court's subject matter jurisdiction is limited to four of the
most serious international crimes: genocide, crimes against humanity,
war crimes and aggression. At the present moment, the Court has
subject matter jurisdiction only over the first three of these crimes.
The Court will have jurisdiction over the fourth crime, aggression,
only after the states party to the Rome Treaty agree on a definition
of aggression (see below). Under the terms of the Rome Treaty,
the earliest period by which such a definition can be agreed is
1 July 2009.

PERSONAL JURISDICTION

Only individuals may be prosecuted before the Court, although those who are under 18 years of age at the time they commit one of the enumerated crimes are explicitly excluded from the jurisdiction of the Court. Organisations, corporations and states are not subject to the jurisdiction of the ICC. This is in contrast to the International Court of Justice, which can only hear cases brought by one state against another, and in rare circumstances can hear a case brought by an agency of the United Nations. While other courts have suggested that certain high-ranking government officials may not be prosecuted while they are in office, the Rome Treaty is quite clear that such immunities do not hold with respect to the work undertaken by the ICC. Thus, any individual, regardless of his or her official status either at the time of the commission of the offence or at the time of the prosecution, may be brought before the ICC.

Military commanders and other superiors may be held responsible for the acts of their subordinates if they either ordered such acts or knew, or should have known, that their subordinates were committing such acts. Thus, a superior officer may not avoid criminal responsibility just because he or she did not engage in the torture, killing or other act that constitutes an international criminal offence. He or she may avoid responsibility if it can be shown that all necessary and reasonable measures within his or her power were taken to prevent the criminal activity, or that the matter was referred to the relevant authorities for investigation and possible prosecution.

In addition to being limited to crimes committed by natural persons, the ICC is subject to a number of other jurisdictional limitations. It is charged to hear only those cases that involve the most serious international crimes and only in circumstances where there is no other viable forum before which individual responsibility for such crimes can be adjudicated.

The Court does not automatically have jurisdiction over an individual suspected of committing one of the four enumerated crimes. To be subject to the Court's jurisdiction, an individual must either be a national of a state party to the Rome Treaty, or the act for which they are being prosecuted must have been committed on the territory of a state party. In other words, there must be a link between the individual suspected of committing the international crime and a state that has ratified the Rome Treaty. If there is such a link, then the Court has personal jurisdiction over the individual.

Thus, if an individual who is either from a state that is not a party to the Court or who commits one of the enumerated crimes in the territory of a state that is not party to the Rome Treaty, then they fall outside of the personal jurisdiction of the Court. As of this writing, a US soldier who commits a war crime in Iraq would not be subject to the jurisdiction of the ICC, as neither the United States nor Iraq has ratified the Rome Treaty.

There is one significant exception to these requirements: the Court can assert jurisdiction over crimes committed by an individual who is not a national of a state party and when the offences are not committed on the territory of a non-state party if the United Nations (UN) Security Council refers the matter to the Court. Thus, the ICC has potential jurisdiction over every individual and territory in the world subject to the approval of the Security Council and the veto powers of the five permanent members (China, France, Russia, the United Kingdom and the United States of America).

ADMISSIBILITY

The ICC's jurisdiction complements, rather than replaces, the jurisdiction of national courts. Even if an individual suspected of committing one of the covered crimes satisfies the linkage requirement of personal jurisdiction, the Court may still not have the power to hear the case. If the Court has personal jurisdiction over the individual for a crime that falls within its subject matter jurisdiction, the case may not be heard if it fails to meet certain admissibility requirements. A case is admissible and can proceed to trial only if all other states that also have jurisdiction over the individual for the same criminal activity choose not to prosecute. Thus, if an individual subject to the personal jurisdiction of the Court commits a war crime in the context of an armed conflict, the ICC will only be able to prosecute that individual if neither the state in which the crime was committed nor the state of which the individual is a national decides to prosecute.

The Rome Treaty mentions neither amnesty nor truth commissions. To the extent that they are used to protect an individual from accountability for an international crime, amnesty and truth commissions may raise questions about the admissibility of a case. If a state undertakes an investigation or prosecution of an individual suspected of a violation within the jurisdiction of the Court, the case may still be admissible if it can be shown that the investigation or prosecution were in fact designed to protect the individual from any liability for his or her crimes. Therefore, the question facing the Court will be whether a truth commission like the South African Truth and Reconciliation Commission (TRC) provides sufficient accountability for violations of international criminal law. If it does not, then the Court may hear a case even though it was the subject of such a commission.

INVESTIGATIONS

The Court has certain built-in checks and balances to ensure that only the most serious crimes that would otherwise not be addressed are investigated and prosecuted. There are three ways that the jurisdiction of the Court may be triggered (or an investigation for the purpose of possible prosecution may be initiated): by a state party to the Rome Treaty, by the United Nations Security Council or by the prosecutor of the ICC. A state party may refer to the prosecutor for further investigation of a 'situation' in which crimes subject to the Court's jurisdiction are alleged to have occurred. Similarly, the Security Council may also refer a matter to the prosecutor for further investigation.

In addition to initiating investigations based on a referral by a state party or the Security Council, the prosecutor may under his own initiative investigate situations where one of the enumerated crimes is alleged to have occurred. The prosecutor's authority to initiate an investigation and eventual indictment is subject to the approval of a Pre-Trial Chamber of the Court. The prosecutor must have a 'reasonable basis' for initiating the investigation. Even if the prosecutor believes that they have a reasonable basis for proceeding with an investigation, they may not proceed unless the Pre-Trial Chamber agrees with their determination and assertion that the case does indeed fall within the jurisdiction of the Court. The decision at this initial stage by a Pre-Trial Chamber with respect to jurisdiction and admissibility is not binding on the Court.

In June 2004, the Prosecutor, Luis Moreno Ocampo, announced that he was initiating his first investigation of alleged violations under the Rome Treaty in the Democratic Republic of the Congo.

CRIMES SUBJECT TO THE COURT'S JURISDICTION

The Court is limited to cases involving the four most serious crimes under international law: genocide, crimes against humanity, war crimes and the crime of aggression. These are all crimes that were recognised and prosecuted by the first ad hoc international criminal tribunal at Nuremberg after World War II.

Genocide

Seen by the International Criminal Tribunal for Rwanda as 'the crime of crimes', genocide is a subset of the more general category of crimes referred to as crimes against humanity. To be found guilty of genocide, an individual must commit certain acts against a group of people with the intent to destroy, in whole or in part, that group based upon its nationality, race, ethnicity or religion. The specific acts that, if committed with this intent to destroy, constitute the crime of genocide are: killing members of the group; causing serious bodily or mental harm to the group; deliberately inflicting on the group conditions of life calculated to physically destroy the group; imposing measures intended to prevent births within the group; and forcibly transferring children of the group to another group. The major distinction between genocide and the more general crimes against humanity is the intent to destroy a particular group of people – in effect the intent to extinguish a class of people from the face of the earth. The intent requirement is simultaneously the most important defining element of the crime of genocide (distinguishing it from other crimes against humanity), and the hardest to prove. An individual's intent to destroy a group can be shown if there is evidence of explicit orders directing that some of the enumerated acts be committed against a group for the purpose of destroying most, or all, of that group. Such intent may be inferred if the killing or other activities are systematic or widespread. As a result of the difficulty in showing this intent, many of the most horrific international crimes will probably be prosecuted as either war crimes or as crimes against humanity.

Crimes against humanity

The Nuremberg Tribunal created after World War II first codified 'crimes against humanity' as a distinct international crime. An individual may be found guilty of a crime against humanity if he or she committed any number of acts as part of a widespread or systematic attack directed against a civilian population and if the individual knew of that widespread or systematic attack. Unlike genocide, therefore, the individual's purpose in committing the act is not relevant, so long as his or her action is part of a larger campaign and he or she is aware of that larger campaign. The specific acts that may constitute as a crime against humanity are:

a. murder;
b. extermination;
c. enslavement;
d. deportation or forcible transfer of population;
e. imprisonment or other severe deprivation of physical liberty in violation of fundamental rules of international law;
f. torture;
g. rape, sexual slavery, enforced prostitution, forced pregnancy, enforced sterilisation, or any other form of sexual violence of comparable gravity;
h. persecution against any identifiable group or collectivity on political, racial, national, ethnic, cultural, religious, gender or other grounds that are universally recognised as impermissible under international law, in connection with any act referred to in this paragraph or any crime within the jurisdiction of the Court;
i. enforced disappearance of persons;
j. the crime of apartheid;
k. other inhumane acts of a similar character intentionally causing great suffering, or serious injury to body or to mental or physical health.

Significantly, the definition includes explicit reference to rape and other acts of sexual violence as one of the many advances of the Rome Treaty's definition over that promulgated at Nuremberg.

War crimes

War crimes are the oldest crimes recognised by the Court and are subject to the longest and most sophisticated definition in the Rome Treaty. The crimes covered can be roughly divided into two categories: those provisions that regulate the methods and materials of the use of force, and those provisions that regulate the treatment of individuals, both civilians and combatants, in the context of an armed conflict. In the first category are prohibitions on the deliberate use of military force against civilians and medical or cultural institutions, as well as prohibitions on the use of poisoned weapons. Significantly, the Rome Treaty does not explicitly prohibit the use of chemical, biological or nuclear weapons. In the second category are prohibitions against wilful killing, torture, rape and other inhumane treatment of combatants no longer engaged in hostilities and members of the civilian population. This category of crimes also includes depriving enemy combatants and members of the enemy civilian population of their right to a fair and regular trial.

Historically, war crimes could only be committed in an international armed conflict (an armed conflict between two or more states). Today, as reflected in the Rome Treaty, acts may qualify as a war crime regardless of whether they are committed as part of an international or internal armed conflict. Unlike in the case of genocide or crimes against humanity, the definition of war crimes does not require that the criminal act be part of a larger systematic crime. Thus, a single act of torture or murder may qualify as a war crime if it is committed in the context of an international or internal armed conflict.

Aggression

As noted above, aggression has yet to be defined by the Rome Treaty but is meant to refer to acts of aggression committed by one state against another in violation of generally accepted principles of international law. The use of military force in self-defense or in furtherance of enforcement actions authorised by the UN Security Council will probably not be included in the final definition of aggression as such uses of military force are widely recognised as legitimate under international law.

VICTIMS

The Rome Treaty provides for victim participation in the Court's activities, reflecting in part the growing recognition of the need to address the effects of gross violations of human rights. Victims are allowed to participate before the Court during proceedings challenging jurisdiction and admissibility. Victims are also allowed to make their views and concerns known at the trial stage so long as it is done in a manner that is consistent with the rights of the accused. Significantly, the Court is also empowered to address and rule on questions of restitution, compensation and rehabilitation. This includes the ability of the Court to direct that an accused individual pay a certain amount in reparations to the victims. These provisions draw upon the experience of truth commissions and other victim-centred mechanisms developed over the last few decades.

State Parties as of September 2004

A
Afghanistan
Albania
Andorra
Antigua and Barbuda
Argentina
Australia
Austria

B
Barbados
Belgium
Belize
Benin
Bolivia
Bosnia and
  Herzegovina
Botswana
Brazil
Bulgaria
Burkina Faso

C
Cambodia
Canada
Central African
  Republic
Columbia
Congo
Costa Rica
Croatia
Cyprus

D
Democratic Republic
  of Congo
Denmark
Djibouti
Dominica

E
Ecuador
Estonia

F
Fiji
Finland
France

G
Gabon
Gambia
Georgia
Germany
Ghana
Greece
Guinea

H
Honduras
Hungary

I
Iceland
Ireland
Italy

J
Jordan

L
Latvia
Lesotho
Liechtenstein
Lithuania
Luxembourg

M
Malawi
Mali
Malta
Marshall Islands
Mauritius
Mongolia

N
Namibia
Nauru
Netherlands
New Zealand
Niger
Nigeria
Norway

P
Panama
Paraguay
Peru
Poland
Portugal

R
Republic of Korea
Romania

S
Saint Vincent and
  The Grenadines
Samoa
San Marino
Senegal
Serbia and
  Montenegro
Sierra Leone

Slovakia
Slovenia
South Africa
Spain
Sweden
Switzerland

T
Tajikistan
Tanzania
The Former Yugoslav
  Republic of
  Macedonia

Timor-Leste
Trinidad and Tobago

U
Uganda
United Kingdom
Uruguay

V
Venezuela

Z
Zambia

Pieces of the Puzzle

FURTHER READING:

Official website of the International Criminal Courts [online].
  Available from: http://www.icc-cpi.int/home.html [accessed
  20 October 2004].
Website of the Coalition for the International Criminal Courts
  [online]. Available from: http://www.iccnsw.org [accessed
  20 October 2004].
William A Schabas, *An Introduction to the International Criminal
  Court.* (Cambridge: Cambridge University Press, 2001).

12 Truth Commissions

Charles Villa-Vicencio

Societies in transition from extended conflict and oppressive rule to the beginning of democracy are frequently faced with the realisation that the systematic prosecution of those guilty of gross violations of human rights could plunge the country back into war. Even where prosecutions are regarded as appropriate, countries are often confronted with an inadequate legal infrastructure to deal with the past according to the rule of law. It can further be argued that the limited financial resources available in the wake of conflict need to be used to rebuild the material infrastructure of a country, including a viable justice system – without which there can be no rule of law. In these situations, the need for prosecutions is counterbalanced by a pragmatic imperative to seize and maximise the emerging chance for peace and social reconstruction.

In these contexts, a Truth and Reconciliation Commission (TRC) can facilitate a measure of accountability and truth-telling from perpetrators, while providing some form of reparations for the victims of the conflict. It can further lay the foundation for the rule of law in an emerging democracy, within which a culture of human rights is cultivated and given legislative priority.

A TRC should not be thought of as an alternative to prosecutions, but as a complement. A TRC need not, and should not, circumvent international human rights law or subvert the demands of international criminal law; in fact, it can and should be consistent with international law.

The International Criminal Court (ICC), international tribunals, special courts, even an efficient national court system, are all limited in the number of people they can effectively prosecute. Prosecutors regularly exercise prudence in determining where to allocate limited prosecutorial resources. In addition, courts are not designed to address underlying causes, motives and perspectives of perpetrators or the role of institutions in the promotion of gross violations of human rights. TRCs are designed to address both of these problems. They demand fewer resources than the courts and, if designed properly, can provide some accountability. They are also ideally suited for exploring historical, systemic, institutional and personal causes and motives for gross violations of human rights.

TRCs AND INTERNATIONAL LEGITIMACY

While TRCs are useful for a transitional society, critics have raised three important challenges to their use. First, it is argued that any attempt to deviate from an obligation to prosecute undermines a hard won consensus that has emerged in the past 50 years, culminating in the establishment of the ICC, to ensure that state actors no longer escape prosecution for gross violations of human rights. Second, any deviation from this obligation is seen to be a violation of a victim's fundamental right to judicial process and the right to prosecution. Third, it is suggested that the failure to prosecute undermines efforts to establish a stable democracy and undercuts efforts to re-establish the rule of law.

While these concerns should be taken seriously, a properly-designed TRC can go far in addressing each of them. First, prosecutorial discretion is an established vehicle to deal with competing legal interests. Prosecutors often utilise their discretion in foregoing a particular prosecution to elicit evidence from co-defendants. Effectively, they offer more lenient treatment to perpetrators in return for 'truth', as was the case in the South African TRC. Second, while the demand of some victims for prosecution needs to be taken into account, this is not the only factor to be considered in furthering the ends of justice and sustaining democracy.

Foregoing systematic prosecution may, in some circumstances, be justified as the price paid to end violence and remove an oppressive government from power. The trade-off is not primarily between the immediate right of victims of abuse and accountability of perpetrators, but between the right of victims of past abuses and the need for future generations to enjoy a quality of life denied those living under an oppressive regime. If a TRC allows victim participation in the process, the right to at least some form of judicial process is met. Third, again as was the case in South Africa, a discretionary amnesty designed to further truth and accountability can facilitate a transition between the impunity of the past and the accountability of the future. Prosecutions can and should complement the work of a TRC, and should eventually replace it once a stable government committed to the rule of law and human rights is in place.

MINIMAL REQUIREMENTS FOR A TRC TO APPROACH LEGITIMACY UNDER INTERNATIONAL LAW

TRCs are proposed for different reasons and driven by diverse motives. They can be used to avoid accountability or prosecution, often motivated by a regime responsible for gross violations of human rights. In turn, TRCs can only be used to deal with certain crimes, either with or without investigation or disclosure of the criminal activity involved. This opens the way for other, possibly more serious crimes, to be tried in court, or on the other hand, simply ignored.

The South African TRC is the one most commentators cite as legitimate under international law. Speaking on the relationship between the prosecutorial mandate of the ICC and the amnesty administered by the South African TRC, the Secretary-General of the United Nations has observed:

> The purpose of the clause in the Statute (which allows the Court to intervene where the state is 'unwilling or unable' to exercise jurisdiction) is to ensure that mass-murderers and other arch-criminals cannot shelter behind a State run by themselves or their cronies, or take advantage of a general breakdown of law and order. No one should imagine that it would apply to a case like South Africa's, where the regime and the conflict which caused the crimes have come to an end, and the victims have inherited power. It is inconceivable that, in such a case, the Court would seek to substitute its judgment for that of a whole nation which is seeking the best way to put a traumatic past behind it and build a better future.

To merit international legitimacy, a TRC needs at a minimum to incorporate the following:

- Convincing evidence that the majority of citizens endorse the TRC as a mechanism of transitional justice.
- The disclosure of as much truth as possible concerning gross violations of human rights.
- Accountability of those responsible for gross violations of human rights, recognising that this need not be in the form of retributive sentencing by the state.
- Reparation to those victims whose rights are encroached upon by any amnesty provision.
- The suspension of prosecutions in a transitionary situation should not be a pretext for the abrogation of other requirements of international law.
- A forum in which victims and survivors may tell their stories and question perpetrators.
- Prosecutions should remain an option both during and after the TRC against those perpetrators who did not adequately participate in the process.

In addition to satisfying the above minimum criteria for international legitimacy, a TRC should also be created and operated transparently in order to sustain democratic legitimacy. Citizen involvement in the creation of a TRC, and an openness to media coverage of its operations, are necessary to ensure domestic legitimacy.

LIMITATIONS ON WHAT TRCs CAN ACHIEVE

Unreasonable expectations for any mechanism of transition may undercut its more modest, but nevertheless important, accomplishments. Significantly, the legislation establishing the South African TRC was entitled the '*Promotion* of National Unity and Reconciliation Act', and not the '*Achievement* of National Unity and Reconciliation Act'. TRCs should not be viewed as a panacea for all the challenges of transition. At best they are one part of a far more complex process that involves numerous institutions, initiatives and reforms operating over an extended period of time. Accordingly, there are certain things a TRC cannot achieve, such as:

- Imposing punishment(s) commensurate to the crime(s) committed.
- Ensuring remorse from perpetrators and their rehabilitation.
- Ensuring that victims will be reconciled with or forgive their perpetrators.

- Addressing comprehensively all aspects of past oppression.
- Uncovering of the whole truth about an atrocity or answering all outstanding questions in an investigation.
- Allowing all victims to tell their stories.
- Ensuring that all victims experience closure as a result of the process.
- Providing adequate forms of reconstruction and comprehensive reparations.
- Correcting the imbalance between benefactors and those exploited by the former regime.
- Ensuring that those dissatisfied with amnesties or the nature or extent of the amount of truth revealed will make no further demand for punishment or revenge.

REALISTIC GOALS FOR A TRC

While TRCs by themselves cannot satisfy the above goals, they can contribute to their achievement. Specifically, TRCs can:

- Break the silence on past gross violations of human rights.
- Counter the denial of such violations and thus provide official acknowledgement of the nature and extent of human suffering.
- Provide a basis for the emergence of a common memory that takes into account a multitude of diverse experiences.
- Help create a culture of accountability.
- Provide a safe space within which victims can engage their feelings and emotions through the telling of personal stories, without the evidentiary and procedural restraints of the courtroom.
- Bring communities, institutions and systems under moral scrutiny.
- Contribute to uncovering the causes, motives and perspectives of past atrocities.
- Provide important symbolic forms of memorialisation and reparation.
- Initiate and support a process of reconciliation, recognising that it will take time and political will to realise.
- Provide a public space within which to address the issues that thrust the country into conflict, while promoting restorative justice and social reconstruction.

A DIFFICULT BALANCE

A TRC process must necessarily promote the beneficence of victims and survivors, as well as ensure that perpetrators are drawn into the restorative process that this requires. These requirements place a premium on reaching agreement over a viable package of reparations, a restoration that seeks to rebuild human dignity and promote the material well-being of victims of abuse. At the same time, a TRC needs to promote the participation of victims in the emerging new regime: politically, economically, culturally and spiritually. This necessarily involves more than a one-off monetary payment to victims. It requires the transformation of the *ethos* that sustained the unjust state prior to transition. Effective reparations require sustainable peace, economic growth and political stability.

Debate for and against truth commissions continues. Not all victims of gross violations of human rights desire prosecutions, while the precise nature of reparations sought may not always be clear. The causal relationships between amnesties, social stability and the rule of law are also unclear. It is difficult to say whether protection from prosecution for perpetrators of gross violations of human rights facilitates long-term social stability, or whether the demand for prosecutions will not resurface to undermine the desired stability. Certainly, the recent history of Argentina and Chile indicate that an amnesty which makes no provision for accountability can return later to disrupt a nation. There is, on the other hand, no clear evidence that the obligation to prosecute will necessarily lead to fewer human rights abuses or provide an enduring process of good governance and rule of law.

TRCs raise legal and moral questions that have no easy answers, but are concurrently an evermore popular instrument of transitional justice. The demands of international law constitute an important foil against which any TRC needs to be negotiated. This said, decisions about whether to establish a TRC need also to be calculated on the basis of political costs and benefits. It is here that the tension between international human rights law and a possible TRC is frequently located. A TRC can contribute to tolerance, reconciliation and nation-building. It can also polarise, embitter and do little more than suspend the confrontation it seeks to avoid. This is why the structure of each new commission needs to be considered carefully while seeking to meet the demands of international law, broadening participation, considering appropriate timing, maximising transparency and political independency, and protecting the integrity and

participation of those involved in the process.

A TRC is not something to be rushed into. It is not the Holy Grail that a society endeavouring to rise above its oppressive past often seeks. Peace-making, justice and reconciliation remain difficult, negotiated options. This said, an alternative to the compromise required is, for those who have known war, often too ghastly to contemplate. It is this that makes peace a possibility.

FURTHER READING:

Priscilla Hayner, *Unspeakable Truths: Confronting State Terror and Atrocity* (New York and London: Routledge, 2001).

Wilmot James and Linda van de Vijver, eds, *After the TRC: Reflections on Truth and Reconciliation in South Africa.* (Cape Town: David Philip, 2000).

Martha Minow, *Between Vengeance and Forgiveness: Facing History After Genocide and Mass Violence.* (Boston: Beacon, 1998).

Charles Villa-Vicencio and Wilhelm Verwoerd, eds, *Looking Back, Reaching Forward: Reflections on the Truth and Reconciliation Commission in South Africa.* (Cape Town: UCT Press, 2000).

13 Traditional and Customary Law

Zola Sonkosi

African customary law is frequently grounded and carried by an oral tradition, through stories and lessons that are handed down from one generation to the next. My own understanding of conflict resolution and the pursuit of justice in African customary law during the pre-colonial era, for instance, was related to me by my late grandfather. Inevitably, my memory of those conversations has shaped my own engagement with peace-building in various African contexts, as well as my own work in European and African intellectual traditions.

African customary law in the pre-colonial era was essentially collectivist. Traditional law and the pursuit of conflict resolution were embedded in group rather than individual rights. In many contexts, focus was given to practical ways of resolving conflict, cultural behaviour and religious presupposition, as much as law. Frequently, the close relationship between these goods expressed a holism that was essential to the form and content of customary law.

A HOLISTIC WORLDVIEW

To underestimate the religious dimension of African customary law is to fail to understand the underlying motivations behind the rituals and processes that compose some forms of African legal practice and statecraft. For example, divine powers are sometimes evoked through ritual as part of calling the clan and community members to participate in the practice of justice and community reconciliation. Thus, to view dances, songs and the evocation of God as no more than an ancillary activity is to fail to understand the essence of some traditional approaches to African justice.

Many forms of African traditional law proceed from the belief that natural and supernatural beings are inseparable. As such, any disobedience to prevailing law by an individual, family, clan or community was thought to beckon punishment from the ancestors, whom they believed continued to live within the clan or community in an invisible form; acting as an intermediary between the clan or community and God. The community needed to understand the consequences of undermining tradition and angering the ancestors (both being seen as necessary to prevent individuals from resorting to crime and other forms of anti-social behaviour). Put differently, the wisdom, values and essential beliefs that were seen to be necessary in providing social cohesion and sustainable governance were embodied in their ancestors and traditions, with any necessary change needing to be negotiated in relation to these realities.

For this to happen, each family, clan and community needed to exist and function within a set of unwritten laws. When conflicts or wrongdoings arose, elders in a clan or community assembled for a hearing to resolve the problem. There was an opportunity for protagonists to state their respective cases. Witnesses were called and the community was given an opportunity to pose questions or articulate their views. Such hearings often went on for days or weeks before being resolved. By the time the final judgment was given, all those with a vested interest of any kind were drawn into the proceedings. Thus, those involved possessed a feeling of participation, if not ownership, of the process and its outcome.

In some societies, the legitimacy of the outcome of the dispute was further entrenched as a result of the king or queen, or alternatively their appointed representative, presiding over the hearings. In cases of inter-ethnic disputes, the rulers of both ethnic groups chaired the proceedings, with active participation of clan or community members being a priority. In cases that involved a community within the larger clan, rather than the clan itself, community elders would preside. In the case of a family dispute, a family elder chaired the proceedings. These events were often interrupted with song or dance in which everyone participated, with some intervals for feasting; all part of seeking resolution. The accused and her/his family or clan were often obligated to take responsibility

for the costs of such feasts. Often, this was seen as an indication of willingness by the accused's family to restore community relations and provided a way for all parties to be acknowledged.

In these cases, liability was based on the damage caused by the perpetrator, with any deed – even one committed unwillingly or by accident – resulting in the person responsible being held accountable for its costs. This repair could range from community service such as building houses or irrigation wells, repairing roads and community centres, ploughing fields and digging silos for the storage of food to the payment of cattle. In the event of the individual perpetrator(s) not having the means to compensate the victim(s) for the damage or offence caused, the tribunal would require obligatory contributions by the family and the clan of the perpetrator(s). As such, the family and clan were implicated directly in the damage or offence caused by a member(s). As a core element of justice in many kinds of African customary law, the principle of collective responsibility was applied for the wrongdoing of any one individual.

Once a verdict was pronounced in any dispute, the King or Queen, his/her representative or an elder chairing the proceedings would not seek primarily to condemn the perpetrator(s) who caused the

damage. Instead, in their judgment, special attention was placed on reconciliation and the restoration of understanding and harmony within the clan, community or ethnic groups, as well as between perpetrator and victim. Victims and communities were, in turn, predisposed to accept the outcome of the process, having been taught in initiation ceremonies and religious practices, authenticated through rituals of justice under the presence of the respected leadership, to do so.

PREVENTION AND RESTORATION

Typically, justice in African customary law has been deeply embedded in the principle of communal restoration, compensation and prevention. The fact that a perpetrator was held as a member of a particular family or a clan was the victim's guarantee for compensation. If a perpetrator refused to comply with the decisions of the tribunal, African customary law provided for the banishment of such a person from the family, clan or community.

In brief, such forms of customary law had the primary objective of achieving an acceptable compromise between perpetrator and victim. They aimed to secure ethnic cohesion and further the restoration of harmony and understanding among the community. What is more, they were not selective. Kings or Queens and their representatives or counselors were not immune from being removed from power for damages or offences committed against the community, although like in any modern society, this was necessarily a contested and difficult process. This said, justice in African customary law had the educational and conciliatory elements that enabled those convicted to play a responsible and constructive role in society after their asocial or criminal behaviour. It was decidedly predisposed towards restorative rather than retributive justice.

People elected to leadership positions in the community needed to be conversant with and skilled in conflict resolution and justice. This needed to be demonstrated through good character, intelligence and proven leadership qualities in contributing to the welfare of the community as a whole. *Ubuntu* (humanness), as discussed elsewhere in this collection of essays, was a basic concept of justice and reconciliation in African customary law. The crucial goal of African customary law was the restoration of peace and harmony within a community by reconciling the victims and the perpetrators. It looked forward to what a nation or community could become, through restoration and healing, rather than backwards on how to punish a perpetrator.

POST-COLONIAL DEVELOPMENTS

Obviously it is not helpful to romanticise traditional African society by suggesting that it provides either a solution to the needs of modern justice or by assuming that it always operated effectively within its own designs. Few, if any, justice systems manage to get that right. The broad aspirations of the underlying principles of African customary law do, however, suggest that insights that are being explored again through Truth and Reconciliation Commissions (TRCs) and related initiatives in transitional justice (such as the Gacaca courts in Rwanda and in other reconciliation initiatives in the post-TRC process in Sierra Leone, in Mozambique and elsewhere) are worth revisiting.

It also needs to be recognised that the advent of colonialism in Africa led to the abuse and distortion of African customary laws by the new colonial powers. Colonial rulers and their neo-colonial successors used African customary laws to serve their own vested interests, a distortion that may have prevented what could have been a natural development and refinement of customary law to meet the challenges of the modern African state. Many African leaders since the advent of African independence in the mid-20th century have destroyed the potential of African customary law, burying it in the dustbin of history.

Evident in South Africa, political transition from deeply divisive systems such as apartheid has created significant tension between the tasks of constitutional reform and the tenets of customary law. In some instances, the premises of the systems contradict, a problem that has appeared when some forms of customary law are shown to disempower women, bar their participation in politics and violate their constitutional rights.

Today, African states have opted largely for Western models of constitutional law. The contribution of African customary law, not least at communal and regional as well as national levels, involves building cohesion and the respect for difference, something sorely missed in much of Africa's politics. There is a need for communities in conflict within nation states to learn to live peacefully with one another, despite their historic and/or enduring conflicts.

For the African Renaissance to succeed, African traditional and intellectual resources need to be harnessed to address the challenges of the continent. Deeply entrenched traditional communities in African states, often unexposed to Western notions of constitutional law and governance, need to be drawn into the ideals of the African Union. For this to happen, African traditions, customary law, historic practices and pre-colonial memory and myth will need to be included in the conversation.

(Written from a tiny rural village in District Municipality of Cofimvaba in the Eastern Cape, South Africa)

FURTHER READING:

R B Mqeke, 'Customary Law and Human Rights', *South African Law Journal*, 113 (1996), 364–369.

T W Bennett, *Human Rights and African Customary Law*. (Cape Town: Juta, 2000).

Thomas McClendon, *Genders and Generations Apart: Labor Tenants and Customary Law in Segregatio-Era South Africa, 1920s to 1940s*. (London: Heinemann, 2002).

14 Human Rights

Susan de Villiers

102   The realisation of human rights requires that people understand
what their rights are, and that they have the capacity to use them
for their own benefit. This means that human rights education must
be a dynamic and interactive process, aimed at educating, equipping
and empowering people to use their human rights to improve
their lives.

In most of the older democracies, categories of rights were
progressively attained through various struggles. Thus a robust
culture of rights may exist, at least partially, in the national law
or even customs of these countries. In newer democracies, where
the culture may not be 'home-grown', or may have been recently
introduced, human rights are more fragile. They can be defended
only if citizens know what they are and how to use them, and when
state structures are committed and capable of effectively intervening
to change people's objective, lived experience.

Human rights instruments operate at various levels. Since 1945,
the United Nations has set many of the international standards for
human rights. Similarly, the International Red Cross sets standards
for conduct in war. Although these provide a benchmark against
which violations can be measured, these standards are difficult to
police if they are not observed by states. A good illustration of this is
the International Human Rights Court, which was introduced to give
the international community a greater reach in implementing human

rights protection measures. However, the Court's power depends on the willingness of individual countries to recognise its jurisdiction. The United States, for example, will not acknowledge the Court, believing that its own nationals should not be tried outside its borders. This weakens the Court greatly. Similarly, international conventions that aim to protect children from conscription are useless when countries permit or are unable to prevent children from being exploited.

Human rights may also be integrated into and protected by national law. In South Africa, for example, a Bill of Rights was included as part of the 1996 Constitution, along with a series of institutions aimed at protecting and nurturing human rights.

Rights are strongest where they are universally applied, to both friend and foe. Thus, it is fairly meaningless for any country to claim to promote and observe a human rights culture if its conduct demonstrates an unwillingness to respect these principles when it takes action outside its own national boundaries. The detention of 'terrorists' in the US facility at Guantanamo Bay is a case in point. The fact that these detainees are apparently held without normal human rights protection is not only a matter for the international community, it reflects the dangerous view that human rights apply only selectively to 'one's own' nationals.

The same problems appear on an individual scale if people's lived experience contradicts or denies them the very rights to which they are entitled. In South Africa, we live in a patriarchal society that, more often than not, does not recognise the right to equality and personal security in the home. In such situations, knowing your rights is simply not sufficient. Children's rights may be openly flouted by families and at the community level. Refugees are often victims of xenophobia and discrimination, despite a package of measures designed to protect them. All these rights become meaningless if the circumstances in which people live make their realisation impossible.

And, of course, inevitably and sadly, the very people who need these rights the most are those who are unable, through personal or social circumstances, to use them.

So we are left with a paradox. The more you need your rights, it appears, the less likely you are to be able to realise them.

CLOSING THE INFORMATION GAP

An important prerequisite for human rights education is to ensure that these rights are communicated in a way that can be understood. Knowledge about what people are likely to understand and able to apply to their own lives requires careful research. If our aim is to reach and teach the most marginalised members of our community, we need to acquire an intimate knowledge of their language, communication patterns, culture and so forth.

Research is important. People, including human rights activists, often assume that they know their target groups and understand how to communicate with them. They are not always necessarily correct. Research into target groups may reveal unexpected problems and barriers. For example, UK research into the way people with low literacy skills look at a printed page yielded the surprising result that such groups do not read what they find in text boxes, as these are seen as containing 'official' information. Another piece of research uncovered the fact that people who cannot read avoid reading pictograms on signage, lest they are identified as being illiterate. This underscores the need for human rights and other educators to convey their messages in ways that are sensitive to cultural and social barriers.

OWNING A LANGUAGE OF RIGHTS

Language issues owe much to the women's movement, which pioneered important thinking about the relationship between language and oppression. Based on the same assumptions, plain language activists have campaigned for the use of accessible language.

Over the ages, language has been used and abused in a way that promotes divisions in society. Indeed, particular forms of language frequently reflect the position or status of a class, gender or profession that wishes, consciously or unconsciously, to set itself up as an insider group, above or apart from the rest of society. In a courtroom, for example, a witness may be made to feel like an ignorant outsider; a helpless victim of the mysterious linguistic rituals of the law.

According to Chrissie Maher, a pioneer in the field of plain language rights, 'Words can humiliate you.' And indeed, how many of us have been ashamed to ask what a document or even a word means because we did not want to appear ignorant?

Plain language activists argue that lack of access to clear information about our rights and duties is in itself a denial of our rights as citizens. We cannot own and use rights that we do not understand.

MAKING RIGHTS WORK: PUBLIC PARTICIPATION

Another way to improve the human rights environment is to open channels of communication and participation between the public and government. An interesting feature of democratic governance in the late 20th and early 21st centuries is an increasing tendency towards public participation. For instance, the African Charter for Popular Participation in Development and Transformation reflects the fundamental right of the people to fully and effectively participate in the determination of the decisions which affect their lives at all levels and at all times. In this respect, newer democracies, such as South Africa, have the advantage over the older and more established democracies. Compared to many others, the South African Constitution reflects a far greater commitment to building the relationship between the electorate and government, and requiring policy-makers to interact with and listen to citizens.

The Ugandan Constitution also guarantees citizen participation in the political planning process. The focus in Uganda is on intervention in budgeting processes, which Ugandan activists see as a crucial way of giving people the opportunity to comment on how public funds are used:

> It is the right of people to know how their resources are allocated and utilised. Budgets are instruments for mobilisation, allocation and utilisation of resources. It is a right for ordinary people, and poor people in particular, to participate in the design, planning and implementation of programmes and activities that should benefit them (Gariye, 2000).

The Uganda Participatory Poverty Assessment Project began its work in 1998, consulting with the poor in both urban and rural areas. The information acquired was incorporated into the Poverty Eradication Action Plan and has influenced budget allocations. In the process, efforts have been made to employ language that can be understood. In early 2000, for example, the Ministry of Finance's Planning and Economic Development set up Budget Reference Groups, and has made plans to create a citizens' guide to the budgeting process.

Bolivia offers an interesting example of the way civil society can mobilise public participation. In Bolivia, public participation is governed by statute. There, the Law of Popular Participation established a national Secretariat for Public Participation with the aim of integrating civil society organisations and citizens into all levels of sustainable development and decision-making. However, the first 'National Dialogue' on poverty reduction and medium- to long-term national development left most Bolivians feeling sceptical about the sincerity of government and the International Monetary Fund (IMF). In order to ensure that their voices were heard, Bolivian civil society organisations launched a massive consultation of their own. The Bolivian Jubilee 2000 Consultation involved more than 4 000 individuals and 800 organisations over nine regions, and culminated in a four-day National Forum on Poverty Reduction in La Paz in April 2000.

Effective public participation depends crucially on having the knowledge and know-how to access public institutions. In the South African Parliament, where committees are constitutionally required to encourage public participation, the public can attend all committee meetings (except those that are, for good reason, closed to the public). Individuals and communities can also participate in the work of committees by making verbal or written submissions.

An abstract 'right' to participate, however, does not ensure that the voices of the poor and the less skilled are heard. In many instances, public participation channels are more readily employed by lobbies and interest groups with the sophisticated skills, expertise and finances to make their case. Poorer and less advantaged groups may struggle to organise submissions, and may be unable to afford to travel to where their voices can be heard. They are also least likely to know about their rights in this respect.

CONCLUSION

In many developing countries, the good intentions of those who draft constitutions and laws do not assure that large sections of society will be heard or empowered. Poverty, distance from parliaments and government departments, time, poverty (particularly amongst rural women), poor transport and communications outside of cities, and low literacy automatically disadvantage the already disadvantaged. This means that most of the work and any available funding needs to support empowering communities so that they can begin to play a role in public life.

State interventions need to include educating people in and out of school, at public events and in the media. They must also focus on the realisation of rights, through the creation and implementation of national laws and practices that support victims – domestic violence orders, land reallocation, welfare grants – and the application of sanctions against violators.

Educating and empowering people about their rights can be hard work and may be costly and discouraging. It is, however, essential to the creation and maintenance of a society based on human rights. Frene Ginwala, the former Speaker of South Africa's Parliament, has said that 'The voices of the people must be heard in our legislative and executive institutions.' Going further, she has wisely noted that 'this will not happen if we sit back in our committee meetings and offices. We need, instead, to seek out those voices and opinions and facilitate ways and means of engaging all sectors of society in critical debates.'

FURTHER READING:

K Y Amoako, Good Governance and Participatory Development (Keynote address of the Executive Secretary of the Economic Commission for Africa). In: *International Conference on Governance for Sustainable Growth and Equity*, Special Plenary Session, United Nations, NY, 28–30 July 1997.

Susan de Villiers, *A People's Government: The People's Voice*. (Cape Town: Parliamentary Support Programme, 2001).

Zie Gariye, Citizen Involvement in the Budgetary Process in Uganda. Paper presented by the co-ordinator of Uganda Debt Network at a workshop on Civil Society: Donor Policy Synergy and Coordination, Glasgow, Scotland, 24–26 May 2000.

15 Rights and Reconciliation

Mieke Holkeboer and Charles Villa-Vicencio

108 Human rights and national reconciliation are deeply interdependent. Human rights protection is about the promotion of human dignity (as affirmed in the Universal Declaration of Human Rights) and about human relationships, a point stressed in the African Charter of People's and Human Rights. This implies that a culture of human rights is not possible in the aftermath of violent conflict without the active and ongoing work of reconciliation. By the same token, reconciliation, even in the modest sense of peaceful co-existence, is not possible among human beings who disregard one another's humanity and continue to commit human rights abuses. While this interdependence may seem like common sense, on-the-ground reality often belies these fundamental truths. Indeed, in societies emerging from extended periods of human rights abuses, 'reconciliation' and 'human rights' advocates are sometimes fundamentally divided in their approach to nation-building.

RECONCILIATION AND HUMAN RIGHTS

Human rights actors are often focused on a principled outcome – a state in which human rights standards are upheld. Reconciliation advocates (including those who work in conflict management, mediation and certain units within truth commissions) tend to place as much emphasis on the process of dialogue that generates a culture of human rights. Likewise, while human rights groups tend to direct their strategies toward systems of law (whether local, regional or international), reconciliation advocates tend to see the limitations of legal judgments, evaluating them as much by their political and socio-economic impact on society as by the degree to which they satisfy strictly legal standards of justice.

Where human rights groups seek to be an objective, impartial voice calling to justice all who commit human rights abuses, reconciliation advocates, while clearly not indifferent to such abuses, place more emphasis upon interpretation and the need to hear all voices, even the voices of those who have committed human rights abuses. Both seek the peaceful co-existence of former enemies and adversaries as the basis for a culture that will minimise the possibility of human rights abuses in the future. Human rights actors tend to see the quest for justice and the rule of law as the critical foundation for peaceful co-existence; reconciliation advocates tend to see mutual understanding and the capacity to live together as the critical foundation for forward-looking justice and the rule of law.

Whereas human rights actors tend to define impunity for human rights abuses narrowly, reconciliation actors tend to see impunity and accountability more comprehensively, as extending well beyond prosecutions. For example, those seeking a fuller notion of impunity suggest that a perpetrator could enjoy greater impunity from an unsuccessful prosecution than from an amnesty application that demands full disclosure of crimes committed. Moreover, given the expanse of human rights abuses associated with oppressive rule, they argue that even successful prosecutions fail to address the full context and extent of the gross violations and abuses of human rights involved. Courts necessarily focus narrowly on a specific set of charges. Other democratic institutions and organs of civil society are needed to address this broader demand for disclosure as a basis for the promotion of justice.

Notwithstanding the importance of effective prosecutions, reconciliation advocates stress the need to address other forms of impunity faced by a society in transition. This requires what the late Chief Justice Mahomed, Deputy-President of South Africa's Constitutional Court, spoke of as an 'agonising balancing act' between the right of victims to obtain legal redress on one hand and the need for reconciliation and a rapid transition to a new political future on the other. It involves balancing what is required for the redress of past human rights abuses with the need to create sufficient political and economic stability within which other concerns – including human rights concerns – can be considered. Ironically, in speaking of this 'balancing act', Judge Mahomed gestured within the framework of a legal judgment (the 1996 AZAPO judgment) to the limits of the law in addressing all aspects of this balancing act. These aspects include the need to redress historical, political, moral and economic impunities, as well as legal impunity.

Advocates of reconciliation are concerned with ensuring that the demand for prosecutions does not undermine national reconciliation and the kind of political stability within which socio-economic rights, poverty relief and other needs can realistically be addressed. Human rights activists are, of course, not indifferent to these needs. In fact, they argue that an unequivocal approach to prosecutions provides a foundation for the kind of stability that is needed for this to happen. They too aim for a society characterised by peaceful, democratic interactions and respect for human rights. The disagreement remains on how to get there.

Related to these different ways of working are contrasting sources of credibility and authority. Within 24 hours of the September 11 (9/11) attacks on the World Trade Center and related attacks elsewhere in the United States, many human rights organisations had released statements condemning the attacks and urging governments to investigate them as crimes. In contrast, conflict management and mediator groups largely refrained from public statements about the attacks, so as not to undermine their ability to mediate among groups with different views about what led to 9/11. Taking their different methodologies and objectives into account, these contrasting responses to 9/11 begin to make more sense. The human rights press releases were an expression of the authority of the international human rights movement, namely its consistent and uncompromising subjection of every human being to the same universal human rights standards without deference to history or context. By contrast, the absence of immediate public statements from reconciliation advocates reflects the authority upon which they depend, namely, their ability to gain the trust of divergent and conflicting groups as credible mediators.

In South Africa, the uncompromising 'no impunity' justice of some human rights groups has at times been a difficult partner within the amnesty-based approach ultimately chosen by the South African people for addressing the human rights abuses of South Africa's apartheid past. Leading up to the establishment of the Truth and Reconciliation Commission (TRC), human rights groups not only provided an expansive database of evidence gleaned from courageous monitoring activities through the apartheid years, they helped to draft the 1995 Promotion of National Unity and Reconciliation Act that established the TRC. And yet, as the Commission moved deeper into its work, some human rights groups intensified the demand for 'no impunity' forms of justice, being critical of many of the findings of the Commission's Amnesty Committee.

As tensions grew within the TRC process around amnesty to perpetrators, on the one hand, and the multiple delays and meager funding of reparations to victims, on the other, relations between human rights groups and reconciliation actors were also put under strain. Reconciliation advocates, while frustrated by the inevitable trade-offs involved in the negotiated settlement and the power plays that characterised the government's response to the TRC report and its recommendations on reparation, nevertheless largely continued their dialogue with the government over how the reconciliation process should unfold. Some human rights groups, by contrast, resuscitated old methods of agitation and a more traditional focus on the courts in the struggle for the rights of individual victims (of gross human rights abuses) and their families, threatening and bringing suit against government leaders and apartheid-implicated corporations. Where human rights actors were concerned with securing the rights of individual victims to redress, many reconciliation advocates were concerned about other human rights, such as the rights to health care and education, and the extra-legal impact that a profusion of lawsuits and prosecutions would have upon the South African budget and foreign investment.

INDIVIDUAL VERSUS COMMUNAL RIGHTS

The missions of human rights activists and reconciliation advocates are generally distinct and unlikely to merge any time soon. However, insofar as actors in both fields work toward a culture characterised by non-violent management of conflict and respect for human rights, they share many of the same challenges. Moreover, contrary to accusations that may sometimes erupt, no arena of concern is exclusive to either field. For example, although reconciliation advocates within the TRC were at times accused of setting aside the individual victim in the name of the larger national community, victims and family members were, in fact, actively encouraged to give expression to their hurt and anger during the TRC hearings and outside of them. While not all victims and survivors supported the demand for prosecution of perpetrators advocated by some human rights groups, those who did were encouraged to attend the amnesty hearings, to have their legal representatives cross-examine perpetrators and, where appropriate, to oppose the granting of amnesty to applicants.

Concurrently, while human rights actors have on occasion been accused of focusing on the rights of individual victims to the neglect of the larger community, they have in fact increasingly extended the scope of the human rights struggle beyond prosecution to promote economic and social justice. Indeed, in these arenas in particular, human rights actors can be said to be holding South Africa's community and political leaders accountable for reconciliation in its most comprehensive sense. For example, the Constitutional Court judgments involving the Soobramoney case in 1997, the Grootboom case in 2000 and the Treatment Action Campaign in 2003, affirmed all South Africans' constitutional right to health care, adequate housing and access to anti-retroviral treatment for HIV/AIDS. The Court found it to be the correlative obligation of the state, progressively and within its resource limitations, to meet these socio-economic demands, steering a middle course between constitutional over-optimism and the demand to ensure the need for socio-economic relief.

These judgments make clear how this kind of court-focused, human rights advocacy contributes toward reconciliation at its most basic level. There is little doubt that human rights advocacy will require the courts to deal with further applications for socio-economic relief in the years ahead. Likewise, as reconciliation and conflict management actors have begun to move from the larger political framework of the formal TRC process to addressing causes of violence and human rights abuse in more 'ordinary' forums and local contexts, they, in turn, offer the building blocks for a society characterised by respect for the rule of law and the promotion of a culture of human rights.

In addition to the productive 'human rights work' of reconciliation actors and the productive 'reconciliation work' of human rights actors, there is a growing field of practitioners and scholars working to bring actors from these two fields into more fruitful interaction. In 1999, for example, the Cape Town-based Centre for Conflict Resolution established the Human Rights and Conflict Management Training Programme (HRCMP) for this purpose. By bringing together actors from both disciplines, this programme has worked to build greater appreciation between them for their respective insights, skills and practices. To human rights participants, training leaders have emphasised the role of conflict management in rights-related conflicts. To conflict management participants, in turn, they have underscored the central role that human rights abuses play in the eruption of violent conflict and the critical importance of securing basic human rights in preventing such conflict.

Because the war in South Africa ended not in revolutionary victory but in stalemate and negotiations, South Africa's transition has contained many painful trade-offs and compromises. But here too there are diverging perspectives. For many human rights actors, the political and economic trade-offs of transition have been viewed as politically expedient compromises that fall short of a full implementation of a 'no impunity' human rights framework. Conversely, for many reconciliation actors, the full realisation of human rights comes not from the uncompromising prosecution of human rights abusers, but from the ongoing delicate balancing of a more comprehensive list of rights and societal needs, including the right to peace and freedom from violence.

With limited resources, transitional societies must seek to provide not only legal redress for victims of gross human rights abuses, but a more comprehensive redress to a much larger population for the decimated social, economic and political conditions that persist long after the formal conflict has ended. Although requiring different resources and approaches, both types of redress need to be engaged.

The reconciliation argument goes something like this: Without a peaceful transition, which necessarily includes a measure of political reconciliation, access to such basic human rights as education, health care and housing cannot be advanced. Given, for example, that the few prosecutions that South Africa did attempt (with mixed results) were conducted at significant financial cost, the question is posed as to whether the financial resources spent on post-settlement prosecutions could not be more effectively spent on a range of socio-economic and other human rights issues not yet built into an emerging democracy. Indeed, even setting the economic costs of prosecutions aside, say reconciliation advocates, the 'no impunity' human rights ideal has had little chance of being realised in the face of the inadequately resourced, under-skilled and frequently prejudiced legal systems that new democratic governments so often inherit from their autocratic predecessors.

Not just in South Africa, but in other countries seeking to build a culture of human rights in the wake of state-sanctioned violent conflict, human rights actors and reconciliation advocates invariably find themselves working side by side. Together they struggle to

balance the needs of the past with those of the future; the rights of individuals with those of the national community; and human rights ideals with what is possible in a given context and at a particular time in the transitionary process. Tensions over different methods and approaches are not likely to disappear. Greater mutual respect across disciplines is therefore needed to ensure that these tensions are more productively exploited to the ultimate benefit of those whose welfare the advocates of both human rights and reconciliation are addressing.

FURTHER READING:

Jack Donnelly, *Universal Human Rights in Theory and Practice.*
(Ithaca: Cornell University Press, 2003).

R Wilson, ed., *Human Rights, Culture and Context.*
(London: Pluto, 1997).

Geoffrey Robertson, *Crimes against Humanity: The Struggle
for Global Justice.* (New York: The New Press, 2002).

16 Economic Transformation

Sue Brown and Funekile Magilindane

The affirmation of the inter-relationship between sustainable peace
and economic transformation is central to any successful transitional
justice process. There can be no lasting peace without economic
justice. There can, in turn, be neither economic justice nor lasting
peace without broad-based economic growth. For this to happen,
there must necessarily be a state governed by the rule of law, one
able to formulate and execute long-term policies.

A seldom-specified prerequisite for economic regeneration is the
ability of ordinary citizens to look beyond immediate survival in order
to plan future activities. Few are going to build, save or put extra work
into anything but self-preservation or defence if they have no reason
to expect that they can retain the benefits of their hard work. As
farmers will not plant if they cannot anticipate harvest, citizens
cannot be expected to help build a new social framework if they
cannot imagine a future without poverty and an endless struggle for
mere survival. However, it is also true that the more predictable the
social framework, the livelier the economy that is able to develop.

ECONOMIC TRANSFORMATION

Peace-building, conflict resolution and national reconciliation are
minimum conditions for economic transformation and development.
The United Nations' New Agenda for the Development of Africa

(Annual Report 1990), for example, concludes:

> Peace is an indispensable prerequisite for development.
> Peace initiatives by African countries should be encouraged
> and pursued in order to bring an end to war, destabilisation
> and internal conflicts so as to facilitate the creation of
> optimal conditions for development. The international
> community as a whole should endeavour to co-operate
> with and support the efforts of African countries for a rapid
> restoration of peace, normalisation of life for uprooted
> populations and national socio-economic reconstruction.

Democracy, good governance, peace, security, stability and justice
are perceived as critical factors necessary to create socio-economic
development. The United Nations Secretary-General, in his 1998
Report on the Causes of Conflict and Promotion of Durable Peace
and Sustainable Development in Africa, recognised that conflicts and
development should not be dealt with separately; rather, they need
to be addressed through a comprehensive framework of governance
that takes stock of the root causes of conflict and charts the potential
for sustainable development.

The emphasis on peace and security as a necessary condition for
development has now become a widely accepted position. In general,
this view presupposes a commitment to:

- The promotion of human rights, the rule of law and an equitable
  social order, as the foundation for national and continental
  stability;
- The assurance that political organisations do not promote
  religious, sectarian, ethnic, regional or racial privileges;
- The maximum expansion of democratic freedoms, including:
  freedom from hunger, disease, ignorance and access to the
  basic necessities of life;
- Overcoming border problems that continue to threaten the
  prospects of peace and security in Africa;
- Creating the foundations of a pluralist democratic society. These
  should ideally include: a Constitution with a Bill of Rights; free
  and fair elections at constitutionally stipulated intervals; multiparty
  political systems; separation of powers; an independent judiciary;
  a free press and freedom of expression and assembly; effective
  military subordination to civilian authority, democratic
  accountability and popular participation in governance;

- The establishment of national mechanisms for monitoring and evaluating the core values and commitments of security and stability.

In a basic way, these gains set the stage for a transitional society to rebuild infrastructure, create stable food distribution networks, enhance trade and cultivate investments. Such development initiatives must be paralleled by attention to building the rule of law and the provision of basic rights, including: freedom of movement, assembly, expression and religion.

THE SOUTH AFRICAN EXPERIMENT

South Africans realise that to fulfil the promise of the 1994 negotiated settlement, the country needs both sustained economic growth and extensive economic redistribution. The broad principles of South African economic policy devised to attain this end is outlined in what follows, recognising that many other countries in transition have neither the infrastructure nor the resources to adopt a similar approach. The challenges and limitations of the South African model are, at the same time, acknowledged as a way of opening debate on viable economic development in states struggling to re-establish themselves in the wake of sustained human rights violations and protracted conflict.

South Africa was, of course, fortunate that the framework of human security, including a constitutional, social, physical and legal infrastructure, were to some extent in place at the time of the first democratic election of 1994. As a result, given a functioning economic system the task of transformation and redistribution did not have to begin from nothing. Despite the democratic government inheriting a system that was mismanaged, skewed and in debt, its transport system, and its industrial, financial, communications and retail infrastructure were well in advance of its neighbours.

South Africa was not devastated in terms of its physical infrastructure of road, rail, communications and storage. Rather, the apartheid regime had devastated the infrastructure of its neighbours, notably Mozambique and Angola. It was here, rather than in South Africa, that one could see lines of burned-out tanks alongside destroyed roads on the way to ruined towns with starving and disabled people. Even the dramatic rise in crime and the drop in human security in South Africa after 1994 elections were not comparable with those of rural populations hunted and literally enslaved in forced labour for mineral extraction in, for example, the Democratic Republic of the Congo (DRC) and Angola.

When the newly elected government came to power in 1994, it identified Black Economic Empowerment (BEE) as a major vehicle for correcting the economic injustices of apartheid, and for guiding the long-term process of economic transformation. At base, the programme aims at redressing the imbalances of the past by transforming the ownership, management and control of South Africa's financial and economic resources so that they engage and include the majority of its citizens. It also seeks to ensure broad participation in the economy by black people, which requires a broadening of ownership – in shares, assets, businesses, houses, land and property – as well as an increase in employment across the skills spectrum and up the managerial ladder.

President Thabo Mbeki has repeatedly referred to South Africa's 'two economies in one country', an advanced, sophisticated and industrialised economy, based on skilled labour and management (which is becoming more globally competitive); and a mainly informal, marginalised, unskilled economy (populated by the unemployed and those unemployable in the formal sector). Unlike many other countries in the region, much of the debate in South Africa has been about the means of including the majority of the population into the existing mainstream economy.

Ten years after the first democratic elections, there is increasing debate over the effectiveness of BEE. It is noted that South Africa is still bedevilled by high levels of class inequality, exclusion of the majority of the population from significant social upliftment and rising unemployment. The process of BEE, critics say, has resulted in an emerging black business elite but failed to generate economic empowerment at the grassroots level. A few individuals have benefited from BEE and became millionaires at the stroke of a pen, the argument continues, while the majority of South Africans continue to be largely excluded from the benefits of government economic policy.

The government itself has observed in its BEE strategy document that despite the economic successes of the past ten years, 'vast racial and gender inequalities in the distribution of and access to wealth, income, skills and employment persist [and] as a consequence, our economy continues to perform below its full potential'. The focus of BEE has focused too much on the shifting of corporate ownership and control, and too little on skills development and education. Accordingly, in 2003, new legislation was passed that aims at Broad-based Black Economic Empowerment; a process that emphasises

job creation and skills transfer in its incentive structures as much as share ownership.

A key lesson of BEE efforts in the past ten years is that BEE is not an anti-poverty measure. It serves and promotes those who are already in the formal economy, or in the middle class, usually by virtue of education. The challenge of developing sustainable policies to better the rural poor, the unskilled and those outside the economy of jobs, companies and contracts is similar to that faced by the rest of Africa's emerging economies.

Looking back over the past ten years, the success of economic policy in the new South Africa is shown by the fact that the economy has continued to grow, without the wild swings into and out of recession that marked the last decade of apartheid. Capital which fled the country is returning. In brief, the success of the past ten years has been stability, growth and reconciliation. The failures are employment, enrichment of the few and education reform.

ECONOMIC IMPUNITY

In the transitional politics debate, talk of impunity is frequently reduced to legal impunity, with human rights purists placing a great deal of emphasis on the prosecution of perpetrators of gross violations of human rights. This focus is both necessary and important, intended to contribute to the emergence of a society governed by the rule of law. The problem is that the focus of prosecution is sometimes to the neglect of other dimensions of impunity, namely those historical, political, moral and economic. Transformation and sustainable peace requires that each of these concerns be given adequate attention. Suffice it to say, unless the economic impunity is addressed through economic transformation and growth, the possibility of sustaining the rule of law and redressing material forms of past suffering becomes increasingly remote. To the extent that the transitional justice debate neglects the economic side of transition, it undermines its own hope of sustainable peace.

Pieces of the Puzzle

FURTHER READING:

K Demeksa, The New Africa Initiative: A view from the Economic Commission for Africa. *Proceedings of the UNESCO-ISS Expert Meeting*, Pretoria, 23–24 July 2001. Available from: http://www.iss.co.za [accessed 20 October 2004].

L H Robinson, Conflict Prevention, Transformation and Economic Growth in Africa: The role of Diaspora. Paper presented to: The City College of New York, 25 February 2004. Available from: http://www.africasummit.org.za [accessed 20 October 2004].

A Sen, *Inequality Re-examined*. (Cambridge: Harvard University Press, 1992).

UN Programme for African Economic Recovery and Development, Annual Report. (New York, 1990).

RESOURCES

SECTION 3

17 National Truth Commissions

The following National Truth Commissions have either completed their work or are in the process of doing so. For a full list of Commissions (including abandoned National Commissions among others), see Priscilla B Hayner, *Unspeakable Truths: Confronting State Terror and Atrocity* (NY and London: Routledge, 2001).

COUNTRY	NAME OF TRUTH COMMISSION	DATES COVERED	PUBLICATION DATE OF REPORT
Argentina	National Commission on the Disappearance of Persons, or CONADEP	1976–1983	1985
Burundi	International Commission of Inquiry	1993–1995	1996
Chad	Commission of Inquiry on the Crimes and Misappropriations Committed by the Ex-President Habré, His Accomplices and/or Accessories)	1982–1990	1992
Chile	National Commission on Truth and Reconciliation	1973–1990	1991
Democratic Republic of Congo	Truth and Reconciliation Commission	1960–2003	Recently established
East Timor	Commission for Reception, Truth and Reconciliation	1974–1999	Outstanding
El Salvador	Commission on the Truth for El Salvador	1980–1991	1993
Ghana	National Reconciliation Commission	1957–1999	Outstanding
Guatemala	Commission to Clarify Past Human Rights Violations and Acts of Violence That Have Caused the Guatemalan People to Suffer	1962–1996	1999

COUNTRY	NAME OF TRUTH COMMISSION	DATES COVERED	PUBLICATION DATE OF REPORT
Haiti	National Commission for Truth and Justice	1991–1994	1996
Nepal	Commission of Inquiry to Locate the Persons Disappeared during the Panchayet Period	1961–1990	1991 (Released 1994)
Nigeria	Commission of Inquiry for the Investigation of Human Rights Violations	1966–1999	Outstanding
Peru	Truth and Reconciliation Commission	1980–2000	2003
Sierra Leone	Truth and Reconciliation Commission	1991–1999	2004
South Africa	Truth and Reconciliation Commission	1960–1994	1998
Sri Lanka	Commission of Inquiry into the Involuntary Removal or Disappearance of Persons (three geographically distinct commissions)	1988–1994	1997
Uganda	Commission of Inquiry into the Disappearance of People in Uganda since 25 January 1971	1962–1986	1994
Uganda	Commission of Inquiry into Violations of Human Rights	1962–1986	1994
Uruguay	Investigative Commission on the Situation of Disappeared People and Its Causes	1973–1982	1985

18 Online Resources on Transitional Justice and Reconciliation

ASIL Guide to Electronic Sources for International Law
Address: http://www.asil.org/resource/humrtsl.htm

Bibliographies on Issues in Human Rights, Berkeley Human Rights Center
Address: http://www.hrcberkeley.org/resources/bibliography.html

Bibliography on Reconciliation and Transitional Justice,
Institute for Justice and Reconciliation
Address: http://www.ijr.org.za/research.html

Centre for the Study of Violence and Reconciliation, South Africa
Address: http://www.csvr.org.za

Conflict Data Service, INCORE – International Conflict Research
Address: http://www.hrcr.org/resources.html

Conflict Transformation and Peace-building: A Selected Bibliography
Address: http://www.peacemakers.ca/bibliography/bib26 reconciliation.html

Democracy and Deep-Rooted Conflict: Options for Negotiators
Address: http://www.idea.int/publications/democracy_and_deep_
rooted_conflict/home.htm

Human and Constitutional Rights, Columbia University Law School
Address: http://www.hrcr.org/resources.html

Human Rights Library, University of Minnesota (available in multiple languages)
Address: http://www1.umn.edu/humanrts/

Institute for Justice and Reconciliation, South Africa
Address: http://www.ijr.org.za/index.html

International Centre for Transitional Justice, New York
Address: http://www.ictj.org

International Court of Justice
Address: http://www.icj-cij.org/

International Human Rights Instruments (Searchable database)
Address: http://wwwl.umn.edu/humanrts/instree/ainstlsl.htm

International Internet Bibliography on Transitional Justice
Address: http://userpage.fu-berlin.de/%7Etheissen/biblio/

Program on Negotiation, Harvard University Law School
Address: http://www.pon.org/catalog/index.php

Reconciliation after Violent Conflict: A Handbook
(Available in English, French, Spanish, Tamil, and Sinhala)
Address: http://www.idea.int/conflict/reconciliation/

Resources on Economic, Social and Cultural Rights
Address: http://www.escr-net.org/EngGeneral/resources_on_ escrights.asp

Restorative Justice Resources
Address: http://www.restorativejustice.org/

Rights International Research Guide
Address: http://www.rightsinternational.org/links.html

South African Truth and Reconciliation Commission
Address: http://www.doj.gov.za/trc/index.html

Strategic Choices in the Design of Truth Commissions
(Available in French and English)
Address: http://www.truthcommission.org/

Transitional Justice Institute, University of Ulster
Address: http://www.transitionaljustice.ulster.ac.uk/

Truth Commissions Digital Collection, United States Institute of Peace
Address: http://www.usip.org/library/truth.html

United Nations Resources on Economic and Social Development
Address: http://www.un.org/esa/

Women's Human Rights Resources, University of Toronto
Address: http://www.law-lib.utoronto.ca/diana/